CODEPENDENCY

A Complete Guide in Learning How to Overcome
Negative Energies

(How to Stop Controlling Others and Start Caring
for Yourself)

Jessie Woodard

Published by Harry Barnes

Jessie Woodard

All Rights Reserved

Codependency: A Complete Guide in Learning How to Overcome Negative Energies (How to Stop Controlling Others and Start Caring for Yourself)

ISBN 978-1-7778032-7-8

Legal & Disclaimer

The information contained in this book is not designed to replace or take the place of any form of medicine or professional medical advice. The information in this book has been provided for educational and entertainment purposes only.

The information contained in this book has been compiled from sources deemed reliable, and it is accurate to the best of the Author's knowledge; however, the Author cannot guarantee its accuracy and validity and cannot be held liable for any errors or omissions. Changes are periodically made to this book. You must consult your doctor or get professional medical advice before using any of the suggested remedies, techniques, or information in this book.

Table of Contents

Introduction

Most people are not even aware that they are chronically codependent? Mot sufferers mistake their codependency for real care and affection. They fail to convince themselves though that their offers of help and care are as well for their partners as it is for them. In the end, they keep rolling in their suffering. Unfortunately, unlike other psychological and relationship disorders and conditions, codependency might not have distinct outward signs. Rather, only you can help decide whether you are afflicted or not.

To decipher whether you are in a healthy relationship, Alexandra Kleeman has a question for you; "Tell me, is there someone in your life who's been sharing your life too closely? A friend or a loved one? Is there someone who's been taking up your time and not giving any of it back"? Answer this question above critically and you are already on the path to true freedom.

What are the habits of codependent people? What are the signs to watch out?

Never say no; codependent people have problems asserting their wish and needs. They also remain highly fixated on being able to help always. Therefore, they are always available to try to help their partner solve any and all problems. It doesn't matter if it leaves them in discomfort or takes up the limited resources they have. They quite simply always want to help, regardless of the situation or their own peculiar conditions at that particular moment.

Do not challenge the opinions of others; Most codependents, especially those with dysfunctional childhoods have been conditioned not to disagree with other people. They therefore wish to be in everyone's good books. Therefore, they would rather keep their mouth shut than be seen as challenging the opinions or suggestions of the people around them. Codependency walks around with low self-esteem, so, codependents undervalue their own contributions to conversations. They may therefore subjugate their natural inclination to challenge the opinions of other people.

Are always there even when they shouldn't be there; it is good to be reliable and trustworthy. It is important to be a pillar of support in your relationships but even love, care and affection have limits. They have boundaries that should not be disrespected lest they become harmful and constitute an inimical object in your life. If you notice however that you are striving to always be there as a source of help even when you should be busy fixing other more important things, it may be time to shake off the shackles of codependency.

Get disappointed when they are not allowed to help; of course, codependents will always get disappointed when they are not allowed to help. It could even bring out a certain violent side of their psyche. They want to help at all costs, so, being denied that chance seems like a hammer blow to them. Do you feel very depressed, angry or extremely disappointed when you are not given the chance to render help? Or when your partner sources for help and gets it from other people apart from you?

Put themselves in discomfort always to help others achieve comfort; well, this is the hallmark of codependency; putting yourself in discomfort always to help ease other people's discomfort. I have emboldened"always"to point out the fact that it is the frequency rather than the act itself that makes up codependency. It is not a crime to put yourself in some discomfort to help your friends, partner or family members. It is only when you allow this become the most recurring theme in your life that it becomes inimical to your own well being.

Are control freaks; this should not be a surprise. Honed by the process of probably caring for other family members since childhood, most codependents grow up used to the idea of controlling the lives of the people around them. They become control freaks interested in all the facets of their partner's life. They want to dictate and help them build their life and actions. They become severely disappointed when they are not allowed to do so.

Find it hard to accept compliments and gifts; funnily enough, codependent individuals, for all the care and help they purport to offer, are very bad at receiving the same sorts of attention. They do not want to be in anybody's debt. So, it makes them considerably uncomfortable when they receive gifts or even compliments.

Become tolerant with abuse and violent; once they stay in a relationship where they are needed, codependents find it hard to cut off the ties of the relationship even when it is gradually strangling them. They may receive abuse, insult and violence but they remain steadfastly committed to the relationship.

Care too much about other people's perceptions and opinions; once again, upbringing maters a lot in this. Most codependents probably worked off their socks to please people in their childhood.

Most of them take on extra efforts to please a critical parent or unstable family members. Therefore, they grow up to be extra sensitive to criticism and the perception of other people about them

Feel guilty for things they have no control over; even in cases where they have absolutely no control over proceedings or events unfolding, individuals who draw joy from codependency blame themselves for everything that goes wrong. A partner's addiction, drug problem or a son's truancy, it doesn't matter what goes wrong. Codependents will find a narrative and suitable angle that makes them feel culpable. This will give them the needed motivation to offer more help and work themselves into the ground trying to fix non-existent problems or problems they contributed nothing to.

Chapter 1: The Nature Of Codependent Relationships

The first stages of a relationship are the sweetest and the most beautiful.

Two people exchange sweet text messages, take calls at 4 am, and have dates with no words said but still happiness abounds.

They feel as if they have never felt so good in their entire life. They feel as if nothing could ever go wrong.

One just couldn't believe this newfound happiness, this feeling of bliss, butterflies in the stomach, and inspiration to write poetry.

A relationship deepens over time as two people share experiences and goals in life.

The deepening of a relationship does not always result to success. Some relationships become dysfunctional over time, yet people stay in it.

They become addicted to the relationship (which they do not recognize as dysfunctional) and they become codependent to the person who does not bring good in their life, at least not anymore.

What causes some relationships to take a wrong turn and become dysfunctional? What wrong has been done in the process, why did it have to happen?

It is a difficult truth that some relationships crumble while some remain strong. The success of relationships could not be foreseen in the beginning.

No matter how "great" of a match two people are, without taking the right approach in terms of building and maintaining relationships, success could not be guaranteed.

Successful relationships are a product of mutual effort, love, and care by everyone involved. This is the same for all relationships –friends, families, couples, groups of similar interests.

But no matter how much effort we put into our relationships, we could not entirely avoid tensions and cracks that could eventually lead to the failure of a relationship.

Where does mutuality end and codependency begin?

The feelings of love, affection, acceptance, and security can be addicting for anyone.

We would all give everything to have it and make it stay in our lives. But how do we know when to stop giving and sacrificing? When does putting another person's needs before one's own become destructive? When does love become a mask of despair and when does mutuality turn into codependency?

People in dysfunctional relationships, especially codependent ones, do not recognize codependency until it is too late.

Codependency wears a mask and pretends that it is about sacrifice, giving, loving, and acceptance.

In truth, codependency is dangerous.

It is an addictive substance that makes a person stay in relationships – even in families – because the person gets acceptance and validation for their ill character or negative lifestyle.

A good example of codependent relationships, apart from abusive romantic relationships, is a family of alcoholics or abusers of substances.

Children feel validated to become alcoholic because their parents are alcoholics to begin with.

On the side of the parents, they cannot "set a good example" and tell their children to stop abusing alcohol because they themselves participate in the practice.

Neither of the two – parents and children – would admit that the situation is abusive and unhealthy.

They stay in the relationship and do not seek help because it tolerates their ill-character and negative lifestyle.

Alcoholic children of abusive parents stay in the house and tolerate the situation because it allows them, or enables them, to practice their negative lifestyle.

How destructive can codependency be?

Surprisingly, codependency does not exactly cause the disintegration of a relationship. Rather, it deepens the connection among people involved.

The more codependent people become, the more they wish to stay in the destructive relationship and continue the destructive lifestyle.

For example, a wife is cheated on by a womanizing, irresponsible husband.

The marriage has become dysfunctional and they are deep in debts and the household is a mess.

A codependent wife stays in the relationship instead of divorcing her husband because codependency tells her that she loves him and needs him to satisfy her emotional needs.

Therefore, she stays with him and ignores the gravity of the situation. Likewise, the cheating husband would not offer a divorce; he is codependent on the woman who tolerates his reckless actions and lack of responsibility.

Is there hope for codependent people?

The most difficult part of self-help for codependent people is admitting that they are in an abusive relationship due to codependency.

They could not see that something is wrong in the situation. They rationalize and justify the negativity that they experience; they say it is only a "challenge" that they will "get through".

What these people do not realize is that there is no hope in the situation.

Staying in abusive relationships, without making amends, could only result to one thing: the detriment of the character and well-being of a person.

But is it possible to get out of codependent relationships or even to avoid being in one? Of course, yes! If you are a self-admitted codependent person reading this book, there is hope for you.

You may or may not be able to fix the situation, but there is hope that you can get out of it, heal, and reclaim yourself.

If you are in a difficult situation and are considering that codependency might be the problem, it is also fortunate that you are seeking a remedy to help the situation.

You are taking the first step towards fixing whatever it is that went wrong in the relationship.

After going through a turbulent ride, it is often difficult to see hope at the end of struggle. When your faith is shattered, it feels as if you could not get it back.

But whether you believe it or not, you are still capable of feeling the love and happiness that you felt back when "everything was alright".

You only need to help yourself and seek ways to improve the situation.

Chapter 2: How To Stop The Abuse

You have been in despair for some time. You have tried to tolerate the situation and "see the good" in it, but you can no longer justify the agony and frustration that you feel.

If you are a student, your grades might have suffered and you are being kicked out from your college.

This time you acknowledge that you have become codependent on your circle of friends that, like you, abuses substances and helps each other get access. You realize that this is the reason you stay with them.

You do not exactly love your friends; what you truly love is the abuse that comes with suffering. You could not leave them because you have become codependent.

The most powerful moment in a codependent person's life is when he or she realizes that codependency does exist in the relationship.

In the beginning, this only comes from the mouth of concerned parents and friends.

The codependent person is hesitant to admit that there is something wrong in the relationship. Denial becomes a way of protecting their interests.

It is only when matters have become too difficult to handle before they seek help.

Get support from friends or seek professional help

The best way to help codependency is to seek support from other people. Find solace from your friends and family.

If you are in a bad situation where you have no one to depend on, there are organizations and concerned communities that are willing to help you.

These people will aid you in breaking away from the situation and start helping yourself.

A codependent person is often the one who feels self-sufficient and can fix the situation through self-effort.

Again, this is one of the illusions of codependency. A codependent person will never truly fix the situation because he or she is addicted to it. This person may think of ways to remedy the situation, but these are all superficial and would not result to any significant effect.

Most of all, the codependent person is afraid to lose his or her significant other. This codependent person will always put the needs of his or her "beloved" before his or her own.

The only way to open the mind of a codependent person is to let others do so.

Always remember that if you are a codependent, your mind prevents you to think out of the box and consider the remedies that would actually fix the situation.

If you already know that you are codependent, you should congratulate yourself because you are on the first step towards reclaiming yourself.

Now, you need to recognize that you need help because codependency is preventing you to get out of the abusive situation.

Isolate yourself from the situation

Isolation from the situation does not equate to ending the abuse, but it helps the codependent person to think more clearly.

This can be in the form of self-reflection or reading self-help material, such as his book.

Isolation is important because it allows the codependent to consider that there is an alternative future, a hope at the end of the struggle. They may not see themselves in a different situation (i.e., leaving the present abusive relationship) but they imagine the situation as having improved or becoming better.

The codependent person imagines a utopia, the perfect situation. For a while the codependent feels happy and hopeful.

But when the codependent returns to the reality of the situation, the more he or she starts to realize that the good fate of the situation is only illusory if everything stayed the same.

This would encourage the codependent to build up courage, initiate confrontation, or seek help from other people.

Another benefit of isolation is when the codependent realizes his or her self-worth.

Far and disconnected from the person who enables or supports his or her negative traits and lifestyle, the codependent realizes that positive character can manifest amidst the brokenness.

This happens, for example, when a member of an alcoholic family withdraws from the situation, attends a rehab facility, and realizes that he or she is better off without being codependent on the relationship.

Isolation becomes a way to realize that codependency exists and only serves as a rotten part of the character.

Address the situation by confrontation

When you have decided that the abuse and the emotional struggle is enough, talk to your partner, friend, or family with whom you share the codependent relationship.

This part would be difficult (first of all, on the part of the codependent who does not want to let go) because it may result to threats, assault, and other more hurtful things.

As you confront the situation, you can bring a friend or a member of the community who can defend you when the confrontation gets tough.

The codependent can start by saying how he or she feels about the situation. "I feel hurt and threatened by this relationship," is a good way to start.

Muster your courage and strength and be ready to leave if the other person does not intend to change his or her ways.

The other person may deny that anything is wrong and would offer to make amends, but unless they are not real amends that would kill the root of the situation, do not believe them.

Show that you are determined by saying that you are ready to leave the situation.

If you agree to fix the situation (attend rehab, renew your wedding vows), make sure that you set an expected period of time for seeing positive results.

Chances are, the situation will become cyclical (they will change and become better in the beginning but eventually return to their negative character), so you should be aware if you are seeing any real change.

When this happens, the best option is for you to find a way to get out of the situation and end your codependency once and for all.

Chapter 3: Are You In A Codependent Relationship?

The initial theory about codependency was first based on couples where one partner in the relationship had a drug or alcohol problem. However, other issues affecting our relationship can enhance codependence too.

We may find that our partner lacks total control on other people's impulses or does not show much interest in the relationship. We on the other hand, go all the way to try to fix the problem.

If for instance our partner is an alcoholic, then taking care of that person or meeting their needs shows something about our personality as a codependent partner. We might be having a hard time leaving the relationship. We may also feel trapped trying to save the relationship over and over again.

Codependency can also occur in some cases where our partner seems uninterested, or self-absorbed. This is normally the case in a relationship where we are the only one who seems to initiate a meeting or the one who always makes a move towards our partner.

It is however important to note, that we most likely find a kind of reward in such a relationship, like when our partner looks out of control and we appear to be in control. We may be looking for respect subconsciously for fixing other people's problems.

The partner who is codependent would be the smarter person, the better person, the person who looks like they have it all together. Most of the time we tell ourselves that we are capable of dealing with every situation instead of realizing that we should be taking care of ourselves rather than trying to prove our strengths.

In essence, there is a high chance that we were raised in a house with people who were also codependent. However, it is interesting to note that people who are not codependent cannot put up with a codependent person for long. Partners who get into a relationship with the notion that love is all about sacrifice and agreeing with whatever their partners want are the ones who are affected the most.

Signs That Indicate You Are In A Codependent Relationship

Ask yourself these three questions if you think you are in a codependent relationship.

Question 1: Is this relationship more relevant to me than I am?

Being in love does have a selfless feeling that might make us want to make our partner happy. This feeling tends to make us feel like we are willing to give everything because of love. However, we also need to realize that we should not in any way be destroying ourselves while giving everything in this relationship.

Question 2: Am I paying a price for being with this person?

Someone with an anxiety disorder can only realize it when they see how much it costs them. It can be, for example, that the price for the partner's anxiety is that he or she cannot fly somewhere fun for vacation.

In that light, it can be helpful to identify a list of the things we are giving up to be in this relationship. If we find that we always put ourselves last, then simply that's not very healthy.

Question 3: Am I the only one putting effort into this relationship?

If our chess partner is too distracted or is not interested in playing with us, then that game is not going to be much fun, is it? This is synonymous with a couple when only one person is investing all the energy and effort.

We might stay in dysfunctional relationships for a long time because we fear of being alone or feel responsible for our partner's happiness. We may also say that we want to get out most of the time, but eventually end up staying. In some cases, we might also even leave but repeat the same pattern in the new relationship.

It can be addictive to feel the adrenaline rush that one experiences when they have a passion for someone. For many people, codependency is the main reason behind their excessive emotional reliance on a partner, i.e. they tend to put other people's needs before their own.

We might not always realize it when we are in a codependent relationship. We might be ignorant of the fact that we depend on our partner to feel good about ourselves.

So what can we do if we are scared or unable to risk leaving an unhealthy relationship?

First, we need to acknowledge it. It is impossible for fear to go away by itself, all it does is to transform into something else. If we sometimes find that we disregard our own needs in relationships, there could be many reasons, but most symptoms are synonymous for people who grew up in a dysfunctional home.

It is interesting to know that most families today are somehow dysfunctional and as such, being codependent is in fact being a part of the majority. Moreover, even though the symptoms can get worse if not addressed, they are completely curable.

We might be fearful of getting hurt emotionally and might even evade a healthy relationship or get in some form of self-protective behavior by sticking to an unhealthy one. We may be feeling like we know only pain; finding comfort in conflict. Dealing with a distant, unavailable, or inappropriate partner might seem something that we like. We might also find a partner who is completely absorbed in us somehow alien.

Codependent relationships normally start in an innocent affair. Two people meet each other's gaze and this leads to a nervous introduction, they exchange names and numbers trying to judge each other silently. Afterwards comes the first date, where they throw each other awkward silences and have random conversations. In the end, they end up developing a mutual attraction and find common preferences. They involve each other in every moment of their lives, and leave their individuality to become a single unit, with the same interests, bed and friends. Before they realize it, what they were in the past has been eroded, and two people have somehow become one.

These first days seem like they are in heaven. Who wouldn't want to have someone with the same likes to share inside jokes, see new movies, make love to, and keep them company all the time, right? However, it is not that simple.

The symptoms of codependency usually develop during teenage years. As an adolescent, we find it more essential for self-validation than even breathing. In order to survive, we depend on factors like: who likes us, how popular we are, and what the opposite sex thinks about us. It is with these years that we measure our self-worth according to popularity, where our ego is boosted according to the attention directed our way. We base our sustenance on acceptance. In any case, there isn't a more satisfying way to be accepted than by our opposite sex.

The adrenaline rush, the ecstasy of first experiences, and the pride of being a half unit are the things from which many teenagers thrive. They feel like they are someone important by having a boyfriend, or girlfriend, and if they were to lose that factor that makes them worth talking about, it would mean that they would have to lose their identity.

As these relationships start to spiral into a downward fall, all rationale is forgotten, and substituted by inane arguments that grow from fear and self-doubt. They start believing that nothing else can make them happy and no one knows them the way their partner does. In the end, they develop a kind of dependency on the comfort and companionship of each other. An addiction to the smell, touch, kiss, and sound of their lover develops like cocaine to a junkie.

These traits develop into adulthood, and all their other relationships seem to be destroyed by their seamless inability to be independent. It becomes hard to trust, because every time a text message goes unreturned or a call goes unanswered, the only reasonable explanation becomes the fear of lying and cheating. The same arguments will ensue repeatedly and their unreasonable habits as a codependent partner will continue to hurt their every relationship.

They will also show these habits in other relationships. They tend to use friendships like crutches for support during hard times, as opposed to mutual enjoyment of each other's company. Instead of keeping in touch every once in a while, they only speak to their friends when they want something from them, but they do not return the favor. When their friends realize this and see that their fair-weathered friendship is meaningless, they will eventually abandon them, and let them rely more on their lover.

They will learn later on in life, probably after much therapy, what damage their actions made them do and the effect they had on their past friends and lovers. They will find themselves wanting to quit the cold turkey style when they want to end that self-destructive behavior in the long run.

Chapter 4: The Codependent Personality

We hear the word 'codependency used loosely. It gets tossed around a lot — there are codependent caretakers, codependent couples, codependent companions, etc. "Originally, the term codependent was developed to describe the behaviors individuals develop when they live with an alcoholic. Today, as we already talked about, the term is often used to describe a person who treats a relationship like it's more important than they are. It's seen with the hopeless romantic who finds themselves addicted to their partner, with a caregiver who puts their loved one's needs ahead of his/her own needs.

Trying to estimate how many codependent personalities there are is hard to estimate, because until now codependency has been typically researched under the context of drug and alcohol addictions. A key aspect of the codependent personality of today pertains to individuals who have relationships with addicts and they are the enabler.

Are You an Addiction Enabler? Enabling is a behavior used to ease tension in a relationship caused by one partner's problem habits. You will rarely see enabling in relationships that are healthy. These behaviors include giving your partner another chance, bailing your partner out, accepting excuses, ignoring the problem, constantly coming to your partner's rescue, continuously trying to fix your partner's the problem.

Codependent individuals tend to find themselves in relationships with individuals who are emotionally unavailable, needy, and unreliable. The codependent individual tries to supply and control everything in their relationship, but they do not address their own desires or needs, which is responsible for the lack of fulfillment in the relationship.

We have already looked at signs you are in a codependent relationship. A codependent individual is hyper-vigilant.

He/she might also exhibit compulsive behaviors that can be in the form of excessive work, eating, spending too much money, sexual addiction, or nicotine addiction.

Sadly, denial is a major obstacle, because it is hard to see codependency in yourself. Awareness is a good start.

9 Steps to Recognizing You Have a Codependent Personality

Step #1 Codependency can take many passive and/or aggressive forms

Terms such as doormat, passive-aggressive, people pleaser, controlling, bipolar, manipulator, narcissist, (drama queen, and many others, all describe symptoms of co-dependency. Stalking is an obvious codependent behavior, yet most codependents would never do this. Fretting over your cell phone in front of others when you haven't received an expected text/call, is another example of codependent behavior.

Codependents constantly judge themselves and second-guess themselves. They commonly live with anxiety caused from low self-esteem and shame. They are constantly judging themselves - what they did say or do and what they feel they should have said or did. Codependents personalities often judge themselves more than they judge others.

Codependent behavior feeds the behavior of a person who is causing pain and stress to the entire group, which can be at school, work, church, social clubs or in the family unit.

We depend on others to become successful in our education, career, and job. Married couples or couples in a relationship rely on each other equally to pay the household bills and to raise the children.

Codependence is not interdependence.

The question isn't whether we should rely on another, or help another person to accomplish common goals that will benefit the whole, but rather the question is are you enabling unacceptable behavior in order to appease the person who is causing a disruption, in order to not be confronted, rejected, hated, or challenged, by them?

Step #2 Examine your family relationships

As we mentioned earlier, codependency is a learned behavior. It is often passed down through generations as a way to cope. You didn't do anything wrong, but it is an inadequate and unsuccessful way for you to deal with relationships as an adult.

You feel responsible for making another person(s) happy, you find it hard to say 'no', and feel you feel guilty for not helping them, but you aren't aware of your own motivating feelings and thoughts.

You may not be aware of your codependency, although there may be constant clues, such as funny looks, which your ego demands you misinterpret, and that leads you to try just a little harder.

Step #3 Examine your other relationships

It's likely that you are unsatisfied with your social-life. You are too busy handling the problems of everyone else, or perhaps you are too busy with work or another addiction.

You spend most of your time thinking about other people - what's best for them, what they should be doing, etc. If someone asked you, you'd tell them that is what gives your life meaning. The trouble is, at best you are unhappy at and at worst, you are suicidal.

It's time for you to consider whether you are an overachiever or just plain driven. You may be labeled 'Type A' personality – you have an opinion about everything, you tend to be a perfectionist and it is common for you to be hyper-aware.

Are you uncomfortable being alone, whether it's for an hour or a day? Wanting human company is natural, but spending the occasional evening alone is also natural.

Consider your frame of mind options. You can rapidly cycle between being miserable and 'over the moon' giddy. Being content is usually a foreign state of mind. In social settings or at a party, you are often the 'odd man out.' You will help the host just to avoid socializing, or you are uncomfortable trying to control everyone so they have fun your way. Perhaps you withdraw from uncontrollable persons. You might escape the confusion, the noise, the loud music, which is actually normal, so why did you show up?

On the opposite end, you might be an attention hog, where you are always in the middle of the crowd or continually on exhibit for attention. For example, you make groaning sounds or noises to get attention.

Step #4 Think about whether you seek acceptance compulsively

Do you often find yourself explaining your issue(s) to someone, or perhaps you provide an unnecessary running commentary? Do you avoid disapproval by hiding your truth? Even when there isn't anyone else in the room, you explain to yourself. Even when you are openly manipulative, you seek affirmation. You expect them to agree it's best for them.

You have created a way to inflict your opinion on others where it becomes difficult for them to tell you to mind your own business. Anyone who saw you as a sympathetic ear, will get more than they bargained for with your manipulative empathic behavior - Let me help control you.

Another common way to describe codependency is that you often don't stay centered.

Step #5 Recognize that even codependents who are aggressive can have a 'doormat' side

In an attempt to be respectful, you may feel a need to submissive in an unhealthy manner. Are you often accused of being double sided with things you agree/disagree on something – wishy washy so to speak. You are an excellent chameleon. You may have trouble knowing how you feel or what you think. You might have trouble with your opinions or ideas if others disagree with you.

Step #6 You notice that you wait for the other person just to listen

You are not looking for real discussion, but instead you make statements. While another is talking, you wait, likely showing your impatience or you insist they stop talking so you can make your next announcement.

Step #7 You rely on others for your happiness

You see yourself demand to literally demand to help another. You might be taken in easily and you might even be seen as a sucker. You have friends that you think of as projects.

Step #8 You need to acknowledge that you are a good hearted person

People become codependent or are codependent because they care; which is still better than not caring. You just need to realize there is a better way for you to care.

You want what's best and in your opinion, you feel that everyone should want what you want and if they have a different opinion than yours, it's not nearly as important. You need to remember that others need to be able to express themselves too.

You tend to be a perfectionist with both yourself and others. It might be hard if not impossible to do anything for you, because you are quick to point out deficiencies others make. Your goal is for this to be constructive, but it comes across snippy and it makes you the enemy not a friend.

You might not take a compliment well. You might reject gifts, only then later you exclaim how you could have used the gift.

Step #9 You only have now

You may concentrate on the past or you may live for the future. You might focus on thinking that life will be better "if… or "when..." but at the same time, you might have trouble carrying out a plan for the future. The idea of living in the 'now' or living in the moment might be foreign to you. You just need to mature and realize that you are good. If you are strong, you can change. You have all you need to fix yourself.

Method to Identify Codependency

Determine whether or not you often -

– Find yourself walking on eggshells – you live defensively, you tiptoe around your own house.

– You are afraid to confront others – you try to avoid conflict.

– You are angry with yourself for letting others get in their way.

– You blame yourself for the displeasure of others.

– You feel used, but you consider that is a sacrifice.

– You get emotionally hurt by the behavior of others.

– You have trouble saying 'no.' You can't stop helping others.

– You make poor/wrong decisions – you accommodate others.

– You overprotect behaviors that are unwanted. For example, you conceal drugs or alcohol for others.

– You tell little white lies so that you can avoid conflict and anger with others.

– Without even realizing it, you tend to over-emote at people. You invade a boundary, you create a negative-feedback loop, you over-emote, and then they back away from you mentally. You come across as inadequate, then you try harder, and you over-emote more... It's a vicious cycle.

– You find it hard to set boundaries on the behavior of the other person(s).

– You feel responsible for the lack of ambition or success of others.

– You find it hard to end a dysfunctional relationship, even when it is obvious.

– You feel like you need to do more and be more. You feel dissatisfied that you can't control the happiness of others.

– You give too much information.

If you believe that you have a codependent personality or that your partner has a codependent personality, you need to move forward and begin to deal with it. The good news is it can be overcome.

8 Tips for Dealing With a Codependent Personality

Start by acknowledging that as a codependent your biggest fear, is being socially shunned, yet it is what you are unintentionally encouraged with these your codependent behaviors. You will attract people to you once they realize that you go about your own business, but that you are willing to lend a helping hand. As a codependent, you can become happier and more fulfilled socially when you change your habits, or when you relate to others in a way that allows for individualization. You need to learn to relate without your ego.

If you cannot interact with them, it will help you if you have a prepared answer. For example, "I wouldn't be comfortable doing that." When they ask you, why not, remember you do not have to give them an answer. Just simply respond with something like, "I just wouldn't." It can be hard in these situations, just try your best to avoid being snide, which tends to make the other person feel justified in shutting you out.

You might want to attend a "Coda" meeting, which is similar to an Al-Anon meeting. Some find them to be very beneficial.

The best advice for interaction with a codependent is simply to not interact! Only then, will there be the possibility that at some point they may respect you enough to ask you why, and you can reply, because you love them.

People who have to interact with a codependent tend to feel like they are forced into telling a lie to answer the manipulative question of a codependent. Avoid doing this, and instead realize you are completely within your right to reply, "I can't comfortably answer that question."

The minute you recognize yourself as a codependent, your life will quickly become better. That's because it seems a mental switch is thrown, and you stop many of the codependent behaviors almost instantly. You give people enough room so that they can be themselves and others are quick to notice. You create a positive feedback loop that will be very helpful. You may still have several codependent behaviors, but you'll start to notice them, which is a huge step.

Whenever possible you need to create arm's length relationships, and keep your concerns to yourself. Listen to the successes and failings of others without feeling you have to be in the middle of it. Create boundaries for yourself, and maintain them.

Is Having a Codependent Personality Really That Bad?

If you are completely codependent it will have negative effects on your emotional health and on your relationship, when you exhibit some signs of codependency it isn't always bad.

Every one of us has at least a touch of codependency from time to time. It is when the codependent behavior becomes exaggerated, when you lose choice and you deny this behavior exists, and so you try to hide your true feelings and you try to ignore that your behavior interferes with your daily living and the quality of your relationship.

If you seek out a relationship that isn't healthy or fulfilling, you may have a codependent personality. However, if codependency is identified early you can fully recover.

Chapter 5: Codependent Relationships & How To Break Free

Now that you know more about how to identify codependency, it's important to know about how you can actually break free from it in your own relationships. Though the task may seem daunting, stopping the cycle of codependency is very possible. There are various steps you can take, if you decide to take the initiative.

Here are many of the most effective measures you can take to recover from codependence:

-Reality Check

The first step you absolutely have to take is to look at your reality and your situation with a realistic lens. Denial is one of the worst enemies of healing and recovery, so sit yourself down and survey your situation and your relationship without sugarcoating anything. Knowing all aspects of a problem is the first step towards solving it, so do so with care. Though it may be difficult, know that you are about to begin a journey of healing and recovery. While you analyze your situation, it's also important that you avoid blaming yourself for what's happened in the past. Try as much as possible to think in a rational way and avoid focusing on things like regret, or things you should have done differently.

-Acceptance

Aside from giving yourself a reality check, you also need to accept the things that you have come to realize about the situation. As with the previous point, denial can only serve to bring you harm. Therefore, the next step you need to take is to accept what has happened to you and to decide how you can move on for the better.

-Recognize Your Role

Though it may be easy to blame your partner for everything that went wrong in your relationship, this is often not the case. It's also vital that you recognize what you could have done differently and what weaknesses prevented you from breaking free of codependency. Doing so doesn't mean that you can now start self-blame. Recognizing your role simply means that you identify what aspects of yourself you can improve upon to strengthen things that can help you avoid falling back into bad habits and relationships.

-Internal vs. External

One important factor that you need to realize is that recovery from codependence is mostly an internal process. Before taking any further steps, you need to realize that you need to focus internally, rather than looking to external sources or other people to "fix" you.

Recovering from codependency means recovering yourself; your values, your needs, your feelings, your wants, and your own identity. These can only come from within.

-See the Positive

A recent study has shown that showing gratitude can actually make a person happier and more content. Though your past may be negative or hurtful, it's important that you try and identify the aspects of your life you can be grateful for. This will help you remain positive, and will help give you hope that not everything in your life is damaged. There is always something to hope for and finding these things in your life can help you greatly on your road to recovery.

-Abstain

Much like any addiction, you need to be able to abstain from what is keeping you addicted. The same concept can be applied to codependency. It's important that one of the steps you take is to try and maintain some distance from your partner, or the person that is weighing you down.

-Safety and Precaution

In line with the previous point, remember to take great precaution in making your safety the main priority. Remember that codependent relationships can easily be abusive. If you are a victim of physical, emotional, or domestic abuse, it's vital that you first determine your "escape route", or where you can go in case of emergency.

If you feel you are in danger or in harm's way, you need to inform those close to you about what you plan to do. If and when you confront your partner, you need to make sure that you have people you can go to in order to keep safe. This is especially important if you have children with you.

-Confront Your Partner

Once you set up a safe environment, make sure that you let your partner know what you're going through. It's important that you are able to confront the problem you are facing and more often than not, your partner is a big part of that. Expressing yourself to a person who has kept you suppressed is not only vindicating, but is also greatly freeing. It is an important step in recovery, and can help you fully move from focusing on others to focusing on taking care of yourself.

Again, however, take this step with a grain of salt. If you feel that you will be putting yourself in serious danger by confronting your partner, it's important that you have people with you to remove you from the situation in case things get hostile. Make sure that the confrontation happens in a neutral place where exits are easily accessible.

-Visualize

One of the most important steps in solving a problem is also knowing your goals and what you want. Therefore, it's vital to visualize yourself in a better place in terms of your relationships and your general well-being. This will also help you recover in terms of getting back to who you are, and getting to know yourself again.

-Challenge Negativity

A common problem that codependent people encounter is having negative thoughts about themselves. This contributes to generally impaired self-worth, and keeps a person trapped in abusive situations. Therefore, challenging these negative thoughts is a vital component to recovering from codependency.

A good way to do this is to question and analyze whether these thoughts are grounded on reality. For example, if you begin to think that you are incompetent, ask yourself what evidence is there if your inadequacy. Did you really do anything to warrant these thoughts? Asking rational questions will help you realize that these negative thoughts are actually unfounded, and that there isn't room to entertain these kinds of thoughts in daily living.

-Stop the Labels

Codependent individuals often label themselves or listening to labels that other people give them. In order to battle codependency, you need to fight the urge to give yourself labels based on your mistakes or based on how others perceive you. When you find labels forming in your thoughts, consciously shift your thoughts to something more positive. Rather than calling yourself "incompetent", change this to something more constructive, like recognizing yourself as a "work in progress".

-Self-Monitor

A necessary step in recovery is to closely monitor your own thoughts and your own self-perceptions. When you find yourself making mistakes or feeling down, respond with compassion rather than self-blame. Think about other times you have been challenged and the times you were able to overcome the various difficulties you've encountered. Remind yourself that you are strong and that you deserve to be free of abuse and codependency.

Self-monitoring is very useful in that you are able to prevent negative thoughts from escalating into more severe forms of depression, or low self-esteem. Keeping a journal of your thoughts can also give you a solid record; something that you can look over to see how you've improved, and to see what you need to work on even more.

-Manage your Recovery Process

Recovery can be daunting, and backsliding isn't uncommon. Therefore, it's important that you take things step by step. Compartmentalize and break up the recovery process into manageable tasks so as not to get overwhelmed. Set particular tasks that you need to complete in a set amount of time. Try to limit yourself to accomplishing that task within the given time, at a pace that is reasonable to you. This will help prevent frustration and will allow you time to recover in a manageable way.

-Seek Professional Help

Though many victims of codependency find it difficult to approach professionals for help, know that approaching a counselor or psychologist is nothing to be ashamed of. These professionals can greatly help you in navigating the murky waters of recovery and can help you sort out what has happened to you in the past. Having an objective party to talk to can also give you a special point of view; one that helps you see angles of the situation that may have been previously unknown to you.

-Celebrate Small Victories

A large part of recovering from codependency is regaining control over your life, and letting the sunshine in, so to speak. A great way to do this is to celebrate the small successes and small victories that you've experienced.

For example, rewarding yourself after finishing a difficult task at work may seem like a small thing, but it serves as a building block to your new foundation of self-esteem and positive self-regard. These all add up and all contribute to building a better you.

-Engage in New Things

Engaging in new activities and pursuing new things will help you get back to your roots and will help you on your journey toward self-improvement. Focus on yourself by finding out what you're good at, discovering what you enjoy and indulge in activities that contribute to your own development. This will not only help you become better, but will also help you recover from the pain of your past. A positive effect of trying out new things and mastering new skills is that these give you something that you can call your own and can give you accomplishments that you can be proud of. Furthermore, these will help you gain a sense of independence that is much needed to combat codependency.

-Pamper Yourself

Part of recovery is to indulge in your own needs and wants. Being in a codependent relationship can really exhaust you and your resources. Therefore, recovery is a time dedicated to taking care of yourself. One way to heal is to indulge and to pamper yourself by doing things that you love the most and reconnecting with what you want outside of your relationships. Remember that you don't need other people to feel good about yourself and one way to do so is to start caring for yourself rather than putting everyone else's satisfaction ahead of yours.

-Contribute to Social Good

One great way of bolstering positivity and feeling better about life in general is contributing to projects of social good. Therefore, try to engage in projects and events that help others, such as a local feed the homeless program, raising donations for charities, etc.

-Reconnect

A common symptom of codependence is isolating oneself from loved ones and support networks. If you've distanced yourself from those you love and those who love you, then know that a vital step to recovery is re-establishing these ties with the people who matter most. Those who genuinely care for you will push you to be better and will encourage you to rebuild yourself no matter how challenging.

-Surround Yourself with Positivity

This doesn't only mean being around people who are good, kind and positive themselves. This also means avoiding situations or activities that are negative for you, such as engaging in gossip. Surrounding yourself with positive things will help your own light shine through and will help uplift your spirits despite the hurt that you've been through.

-Express Yourself

Whether it be to your counselor, your family or your friends, it's important that you fully express what you're feeling and what you've been through. Keeping everything to yourself inevitably becomes a heavy burden, so lighten your life by telling others what you've been through and what you are going through. Know that you aren't alone, by sharing the burden with other people can make you feel more hopeful and motivated to move on.

-Assert Yourself

Though this is easier said than done, it's important that you take small steps to ease into the practice of asserting yourself, your opinions and who you are. This will help you realize that you can do things of worth and that you always have something valuable to contribute.

For example, you can take control of small projects at work; whether this is decorating the office for Christmas parties or complex strategic planning of business goals.

-Religion & Spirituality

If you are a religious or spiritual person, these are actually positive factors that contribute to your recovery. Some studies have shown that religion, prayer and spirituality are actually factors that contribute to emotional resilience and wellbeing. Therefore, when recovering from codependency, try and reconnect with your religious or spiritual roots to bolster your recovery process.

-Physical Wellness

Physical, mental and emotional wellness are interconnected. Therefore, when trying to recover from codependency, it's important that you don't overlook your physical health. A good way to feel better and recover from codependence is to invest time into exercise and to maintain a healthy lifestyle. Being active by exercising will help you feel better about yourself, and will also help you boost your self-image and self-esteem.

-Trust Your Feelings and Intuitions

Codependent people often suppress their own instincts, even though what they feel inside may be telling them that what they're doing is not in line with their authentic selves. Recovery means that you have to learn to trust yourself again; trust yourself to know what's good for you and to know what's bad for you. You don't have to immediately tackle complex tasks; start small and work your way from there.

-Create a Positive Sanctuary

Aside from internally bolstering your sense of positivity, it's also helpful to make a space that you dedicate solely for relaxation and positive activities. You can come to this place everyday to simply relax and to do things that you love. This can be anything from physical activities like yoga or meditation, to simple hobbies like reading or listening to your favorite music. When things get too stressful, make sure that this can serve as your sanctuary of safety and positivity.

-Have A Stress-Release Session

Frustration and stress are part of the course when you're on the road to recovery. Your tendency may be to suppress these feelings, but a better way to manage them is to set a time for you to release all your stress and frustration.

For example, setting half an hour a week to cry, to vent and to allow yourself to feel negative will help diffuse your tension and to prevent a possible breakdown. However, be sure that you don't allow yourself to go beyond this "session". Allow yourself only this time and move on afterwards.

-Start the Day With Commitment

The road to recovery requires you to make a decision and a commitment to making yourself better. However, decision and commitment to heal isn't made only once. You need to make it continually and to keep reminding yourself that recovery is your main priority. Therefore, start your day right by constantly making and repeating your commitment to yourself despite the odds.

-Believe in Yourself

One of the most vital aspects of recovery is believing that you can do it, and believing that you can defeat codependence. Remember that you are in charge of your own fate, and that you have control over your own life and how you want to live it. Nobody deserves to be abused and nobody deserves to be made to feel small or worthless. Always keep in mind that you are valuable, unique and worthy of love. Keeping all these thoughts at the forefront will help you see your journey through and will help you engage in relationships that are better for you.

Chapter 6: Food And Work As Co-Dependency Parameter #4

Addiction to Food in Co-dependency

Food enablers are the co-dependent factors of increasing or adding to one's obesity or overeating disorders. Co-dependent partners that can add to one's eating disorders can be the parent, the kids, the partners or the friends. Due to the aforementioned harmful effects of co-dependency, some of the emotional imbalances of anxiety, restless, hypersensitivity, depression and stress can add to venting out the same through over-eating.

Spouses of the food-a-holics will try to please their partners by cooking exotic delicacies that render the subject and the partner to become obese on their own. Even though the co-dependent tries to limit the food intake of the partner and put down rules of healthy food diets, the love and other factors of co-dependent makes them the food enablers that lead to the obesity of both, in the due time. One's lack of communication and other misunderstanding inclusive of the intimacy issues can pull the reasons for venting out the aspects of anxiety through eating. Co-dependents should instead show the delight of delicacy through healthy diet.

Another theory of psychology dictates that co-dependency itself arises from a family dysfunction of overeating or obesity. When someone in a family has the habit of overeating, the children and other family members are also invited to the sumptuous dining, everytime the food addict has a rush or pang, hence inducing the same overeating disorder in the rest of the family. This also teaches the family that overeating is a pleasant vent out or resolution for one's anxieties depression and stress.

Workaholics as part of co-dependency Parameter

Do you feel that the undue business tours and official appointments of our partner is leaving you lonely, unsatisfied, compromised and confined without any bliss in your relationship? Then your co-dependency is largely dependent on your partner's workaholic nature.

Workaholism is one of the biggest cause and effects of maintaining stability in a family, A workaholic patriarchal or simply, the head in a family enables the rest of the family to feel incomplete and discontent with the time spent with the workaholic. This induces a dissatisfactory co-dependence on account of the subject. They tend to adjust, compromise and fake affection to mask the absence and dissatisfaction with the concerned workaholic. Gradually, the rest of the family grown into a dysfunction of perspective that work is the only duty one should regard and respect. This instils a sense of detachment with morals, humanity, warmth and family values as each individual member of the family grows to regard their work of utmost importance.

Exemplifying, a highly workaholic businessperson father or mother can instil in their kids a sense of loneliness, detachment and ideology that is centred on the belief of delivering just productivity, money and profit as the morals of their life. The kid learns to regard his work more than his own family, and hence run to work even at his li'l girl's deathbed.

Friendships as Co-dependency Parameter #5

Friendship is one of the easily manipulative settings of inducing co-dependency on account of hopelessness, loneliness and other insecurities or complexes.

Do you feel like your best friend is trying to steal your boyfriend, which she is flirting past limits with your boyfriend that you are paranoid and stressed out by the same? Do you feel that your best friend suddenly behaves weird around your other friends that you have to separately meet your best-friends and other buddies? Do you feel that your best friend is taking decisions for you without even consulting you? Do you feel that your best friend emotionally threatens to disclose sensitive data to your parents or siblings, if you take certain decisions? Does your best friend excuse draining your time of celebration and exhilaration by precisely interfering in your personal space repeatedly?

Then, it is time you realised that you are a prey to a strong co-dependent friendship. Co-dependent friendship accounts to draining a person's emotional balance, peace, calmth and sanity in almost all circumstances!

1)   Chaos: an important aspect of co-dependent friendship is through inducing chaos in the relationship through various methods. This involves the co-dependent behaving in irrational ways and other expressions to make unnecessary issues and undue chaos amongst the group. Chaotic situations fuel the subject's power of emotional control over the person, as the other focuses on relieving the co-dependent from the misery.

2)   Melodrama: another important aspect of co-dependent friendships is that induces   repeated   melodramatic

circumstances to resolve the focus of the group back to the co-dependent and his or her authority over the partner's act of friendships.

3)		Saviour: another important aspect of co-dependent friendships is the demeanour of being a saviour. The saviour identify of co-dependents is that they are highly motivated to take care of the other and protect them from every risk and unexpected happenings that they feel like it is their duty that can result in saving or destroying their friend's life.

4)		Giver and not the Receiver is one of the most harmful effect of a co-dependent friendship that relies on giving the friend all of one's self-sabotages, respect and sacrifices to receive nothing in return but constant motivation to give more! This is the aspect of endless giver who neither is appreciated, nor rewarded for the same.

Inducing false values about other friends is another heavily strong aspect of co-dependent relationships. A co-dependent friend will infiltrate the partner's mind with many false stories of inducing a negative judgement about the rest of the friends. This involves backbiting about other friends and creating false stories that demean the other, being told as other friend's judgements to induce isolation in the partner. This isolation arises due to the fear of the subject, which compels him or her to make false stories to safeguard the friendship. Selflessness is the ultimate signal to spot a poor co-dependent friendship.

Here, your friend's dreams, values, demands and desires hold a threat to your own desires and comforts and you end up being the embodiment of selflessness that exists by de-valuing your own commitments, desires and ambitions. A co-dependent friendship ends up harming one partner rather than helping, comforting or inducing productivity in the relationship.

Narcissist as a Co-dependency Magnate or Parameter #6

When a co-dependent personality and a narcissist come together, it is the perfect satisfied puzzle. In this case, a narcissist becomes a magnet for the co-dependent. A co-dependent person is deeply enthralled and excited to share the company of a narcissist because the narcissist makes the best partner for the co-dependent for follow. A narcissist is not diseased but a caregiver to the addicted. When the addict is addicted to his or her own self, then the role of a co-dependent partner seems to fuel all aspects of narcissism by diminishing the respect for the subject's self, confidence, respect and abilities.

A narcissist's love for himself is what attracts the co-dependent personality to relieve her or his own duties to make way for ways of worshipping the narcissist. This grows into such a setting that the subject even becomes the cause of the partner's self-destructive behaviour. As co-dependents as endless givers, a narcissist drains all the passion and energy out of them, to make the other happy and content. They are stuck inside the pattern of perpetual giving rather than any receiving. In this moment, pessimism and discontent with the self arises, to induce a feeling of constant feeling of jadedness and incapability in the co-dependent. As a narcissist never values other's feelings more than their own selfishness, a co-dependent compromises, adjusts and relies on making sacrifices to pleasures the narcissist, who does not regard any of this the slightest acknowledgement, lest appreciation.

A narcissist on the other hand is happy with this symbiotic relationship of them having the power to lead and command the co-dependent, who is more than happy to follow the narcissist. The attraction is strong at the start but highly diminishes with due time. The co-dependent easily buys the dysfunction being part of their own disability, incapability and flaws, by comparing themselves with the narcissists. In this case, the confidence and self-respect levels of both are immensely different as the former has extremely low self-respect while the other has the highest self-respect for the self.

Ultimately, the co-dependent reaches a point where his or her own desires are not voiced upon fearing heavy rejection and embarrassments of losing the narcissist if voiced. Additionally, another category of narcissists, also known as inverted narcissists to whom the profit or usefulness of the co-existence and co-dependency makes an impact only through a narcissistic exhilaration of the self.

Facing the Hard Reality

Dealing with a loved one who has a serious addiction is not always easy. But this is one of the most important steps for you to take in order for you to "survive" when living with an addict. You must realize that just because you may wish your loved one's addiction will just go away doesn't mean that is will magically disappear. You are going to have to come face-to-face with the hard reality of your loved one being an addict. The addictive behaviour your loved one has may include drugs, alcohol, an eating disorder, or perhaps compulsive gambling.

Don't Feel Guilty for Saying No.

You must not feel guilty for refusing or saying no to your addicted loved one if they are asking something of you that you do not feel comfortable with. If they are asking you for money do you just give it to them in hopes that they will be happy and won't cause anymore mental or perhaps physical abuse towards you? Whatever your reasons are, in your heart you know this is not going to get better and instead as their addiction progresses things will just get worse for you and for them. You must learn to stand strong by saying no and standing by that decision.

Your loved one will try and make you feel guilty in some way in hopes that you will give in and perhaps give them the money they want to feed their addiction. In order to help them you must teach them that "No means No" and that you will not be bullied into changing your mind. Addicts become very good at making their loved ones help them out in one way or another by manipulating them into doing things for them. Remember that sometimes you have to be cruel to be kind.

Take Care of Yourself.

It is very important that you make sure to take care of your own health instead of always trying to help your loved one with the addiction. If you don't take care of your own health you will eventually burn out and you won't be able to help others like you like to do. Don't let your addicted loved one totally run your life so that you are spending all your time seeing to their needs and not your own. You need to spend time doing things to better your own life; try and get involved with things that you actually enjoy doing.

Perhaps you might want a change of career or maybe you want to go back to school. The world is your oyster but you have to walk out and get involved with the world beyond the addict in your life. Don't make your life and world revolve around them. You have to realize that you cannot change him/her;they have to want to get help for themselves. You cannot fix someone who does not want to be fixed; unless they want the help there is nothing you can do.

You are only responsible for your own actions. You can help your loved one by refusing to be an enabler any longer. Let them know that you are willing to support them and help when they decide to get help for their addiction. But let it be clear to them that you will no longer be an enabler for their addiction. You must learn to stop helping the addict in your life in anyway that is going to help them to continue with their addiction instead of them seeking treatment. No matter how bad you will be made to feel at times by the addict you must remain firm on your decision not to continue to be an enabler.

They have to know that your are serious and mean what you say in that "no means no."

Addiction Affects Your Quality of Life

You must think of your own health and well-being first and foremost. Your loved one's addiction is not only going to lessen the quality of their life but it is also going to affect the quality of your life in a negative way also. The difference between the two of you is that they made the choice to bring this addiction into their life and you on the other-hand did not. But because of poor choices your loved one has made, they are causing you suffering in your life too. You may be isolated from other loved ones because they or perhaps you don't want them to see "the addict" that you love and are trying to protect.

Embarrassed and Ashamed that You Love an Addict

You might feel embarrassed and ashamed of your life loving an addict so you try avoiding other friends and family members so they do not have to see how bad the quality of your life has become. You constantly come up with excuses for why your addicted loved one is not at any family functions or any other gatherings with you. You don't invite other loved ones to your home but try and discourage them from coming there. Instead you might agree to meet them at a restaurant for lunch.

Stop Denying that Anything is Wrong

You try and convince others that your life is just fine and that your partner just isn't real sociable but is the quiet stay at home type. Family and friends believe the addict you love has nothing in common with you and they don't understand why or what you see in this person. You try and tell others that you are opposites and that is why you are attracted to one another. You say to them haven't you ever heard of "opposites attract?"

You tell them you prefer to get out of the house and visit with them. But they notice changes in you and they sense that not all is as well as you are trying to portray it to be. What you really need to do is stop protecting the addict and your denial that anything is wrong. You must look at what is going on in your life and ask yourself why it is happening and what you are doing to make it worse or better.

Prepare to Get Help for You Both

You should seek some support either from close family, friends, counselling or a mixture of all these support resources. You need to stop living in denial of your loved one's addiction and accept it and that you need to seek help and guidance on what you can do to make your life better. In order for you to move forward in your life, you are going to have to come to terms with the reality of your situation in that you are living with and love a person with an addiction. In order for you to help yourself and your loved one, you are going to have to make some serious choices on how you are going to approach getting the help that you both so desperately need to help make your lives healthier than the ones you are both currently living.

You Must be Strong Minded

You are going to have to be the strong-minded one in order to do what is right in seeking help for you both. Your addicted loved one may fight you on making a decision towards seeking help. They may try to guilt you out of it by manipulating you; this is something that most addicts are very good at doing in order to keep their addiction going for as long as possible.

They may curse at you, scream and cry begging you to have mercy and forget this idea of getting help. They may say to you that if you really truly love them you will not do this.

Seeking Help Even if Addicted Loved One Does Not

The addict in your life may not be ready to change or seek help. They will make many excuses to you why they can't or are not ready at that particular point in time to go into treatment and get the help they need. You must be strong and put your foot down and say,"no more excuses, we start today with getting the help we need to get rid of this addiction that is affecting both of our lives". If they refuse to be part in seeking help you must still get help and support for yourself in learning what you can do to improve your situation. It is important that you get support from an outside source that can help to give you advice on things that you should try and do in order to improve the quality of your life.

The important thing to do is try and make sure that you are doing things that will keep you healthy during these trying times in your life. In order for you to stay strong you must start making healthy choices for yourself so that you do not succumb to the stress and anxiety you are dealing with while living with an addict.

Chapter 7: How To Tell You're In A Codependent Relationship

By now, you may recognize that you are in a codependent relationship. You may rely heavily on one friendship in particular, or pay extra attention to your spouse. It is natural to gravitate toward certain people, so don't overanalyze every relationship you are in. Still, it important to take stock of your relationships and begin to recognize if you are being used, or if you are using someone else. There are two sides to this equation, and it is important to establish healthy boundaries with friends and loved ones.

How do you know if you are being used? This one should be pretty simple to spot, but not always. Take inventory of your friends. Is there someone who consistently calls you for help with things? Looking after their kids? Getting yard work done? While you may be happy to help, is that person reciprocating the favors? If that person comes to rely on you to babysit, but never helps with your kids, or simply expects it from you, it may be time to set some boundaries. While that person may not be able to reciprocate in an appropriate manner, they should at least be grateful, and be cognizant of your time and energy.

In a spousal relationship, this may be harder to spot. In any relationship, roles are established early on. An over-eager spouse may want to take care of their loved ones every need, offering to cook, clean, wait on them hand and foot. While this may seem like a way to show affection, it can quickly turn into a codependent relationship. Unless the partner can reciprocate in some way, it may seem like the relationship is very one-sided. Over time, the over-eager spouse will become tired and a bit resentful that their partner is taking advantage of their good nature. However, by this time, they may feel like their self-esteem is reliant on how their spouse feels about them, likely a habit they developed earlier in life.

Being used can have many definitions. Someone may rely on you financially, or for help getting places if their car is broken. Your intentions are likely good, and just doing favors for someone doesn't mean you are codependent. You may be, however, if you start going out of your way, putting your own life on hold, to help someone else, especially when it is out of guilt. This is the ultimate definition of being used. Often times, if you are reliable and always there for someone, the moment you are not may make you feel guilty. This guilt could stem from your own feelings of inadequacy, or from the person you constantly help to make you feel guilty. Either way, the relationship has escalated to an unhealthy level, and it is time to set some boundaries. Yes, boundaries are discussed a lot, we will get to how to manage these relationships later on in the book.

This may be particularly difficult to pinpoint if a relationship has been this way most of your life. Of course, we are talking about a long-standing relationship between an adult child and their parents. It is important to stay in touch and take care of the people who raised you, but that relationship can get out of control as well. For example, let's say you suspect you may be in a codependent relationship with your own mother. In this case, your parents are divorced, and your mom lives on her own. She is constantly calling you to help mow the lawn and do daily tasks for her. You begin to forgo your own responsibilities to be at her beckoned call. One day, you decide to take a day trip with your own kids. Mom calls first thing in the morning and asks for help with something at her house. You explain that you are going out, but your mother makes you feel guilty, saying things like, " I only raised you", or "If it doesn't get done now, it will never get done", anything to make you feel guilty for having your own life. This type of relationship develops over time and is usually the result of codependency starting from early childhood. Your mother may not have had successful relationships in her past, specifically with her parents, and is bringing that to the relationship with you.

We often see this sort of relationship between mothers and their daughters in law. TV shows and movies have been dedicated to these relationships, in which the mother believes that nobody can take good care of her son, and anybody who tries is doomed to disappoint her. The mother is dependent on her son needing her for her own self-worth. Once she realizes that her son is grown and does not depend on her, she may lash out at his significant other, or the son, making both parties feel guilty for not spending more time.

How do you know if you are the user? Again, take stock of the relationships you are currently in. Is there one friend you always rely on to bail you out? Do you ever pay back the favor, or are you accustomed to them helping you? Another big one, do you feel upset when that person cannot help and do you give them an attitude, or act ungrateful when they can't step away?

In your personal relationship, do you expect your significant other to be with you all of the time? If they want to spend time with friends do you get jealous or upset? Do you make them feel guilty when they hang out with other people? These things may be difficult to face, and if they are, it is a good indicator that you are in a codependent relationship. If this sounds like you, it may mean that your self-esteem has been dictated by relationships like this in the past. It doesn't mean that this cannot be changed.

Perhaps one of the most difficult codependency relationships to deal with is one with addiction involved. If you are involved with someone with a drug addiction, gambling habit or something similar, it is likely that this person was not this way when you entered the relationship. Had you met them on the street in their current state, these facts would have been a major red flag for you to step away. Unfortunately, that person you are in love with was once a different person, and was not on drugs, or spending every night at gambling at the casino.

It is hard to come to terms with letting this relationship go because you see what was, and what potential is there in this person. Instead, you let the dysfunction continue, hoping that eventually, the person you knew and loved will come to their senses. This is exactly what happens with parents of drug addicts as well. Their sweet son or daughter is in there somewhere, and they are very susceptible to being manipulated by that person. That person will become dependent on their willingness to help, while their loved one becomes guilted into continuing to help them. Unfortunately, this just enables bad habits and the likelihood that they will snap out of it on their own is slim to none. If you make it easy for a drug user to continue abusing drugs, they don't have a good reason to stop.

Chapter 8: 5 Ways To Be Codependent No More

There are many ways that can help you overcome codependency. However, we will only focus on a few that if applied properly and with consistency, can have a great impact on the quality of your relationships and eventually your life.

1# Make boundaries

We may be the kind of person who can feel what other people actually want even before they say it by simply being intuitive. However, if we cannot say no to what they want us to do, we are codependent, which means we will definitely not be living our life to the fullest. One of the most important things to know when we are learning how to stop people pleasing is to develop personal boundaries. We can start by learning when to say no and where to draw the red line.

A good example would be not allowing our self to be convinced by someone else to do something we don't want to do, even if they manipulate us with negative comments. We cannot change what other people do but we can change how we respond to their actions. Setting these boundaries will help improve our relationships.

2# Listen to your own feelings and trust your intuition

We might have grown up learning to feel guilt and shame frequently. We learned to say sorry and give an explanation even when we truly felt that we did not have to. When you come out of that restricted world, you will begin to take responsibility of your own feelings. Look deeply into your feelings and thoughts and remind yourself that you are entitled to opinions and judgments. With that, you will not feel under pressure to impress anyone.

3# Honor your own intentions and needs

While growing up, we probably made decisions depending on what other people wanted without actually improving ourselves. We might have felt afraid even before we would say a word. In order to realize what you are feeling, you must start by questioning the motive behind your words and actions. This will allow you to understand your own motives and ideas, rather than letting other people decide them for you. It helps to develop a sense of self-respect and confidence, making it easier to interact with others and not feel sorry for whatever you want to do.

4# Establish a positive space

Feeling responsible for other people's thoughts, actions, and reactions can leave you confused and drained. When you start to realize the difference between bearing other people's problems and showing them support, you can start to create your own positive space. This is what boundaries is all about; knowing where you end and where someone else starts.

You need to realize that you do not need to be responsible for other people. For instance, if someone has not called you back after leaving three voicemails, it is not your fault, and it is definitely not up to you to get them to call you back. Likewise, if there is a pause in a conversation, it is not your responsibility to resume it.

There is a healthier way to accept how other people are and arrange the given pieces by not trying to make up for them.

5# Focus on raising your self-esteem and confidence

There is a saying that goes "The more you know yourself and what you want, the less you let other things frustrate you". There could be no other truer words. Ultimately, you are responsible for yourself and your own happiness. What you make yourself to become is what you probably transfer to others. In this ever-changing and spontaneous world, when you learn to love yourself, you will not only grow stronger but also strengthen the people around you.

Chapter 9: How To Avoid Codependent Relationships

Prevention is better than cure. This is true not just in medicine, but also in relationships. As you enter a new relationship, it feels as if everything falls into place.

You could not foresee any difficulties or tendencies that it might become an abusive, codependent relationship.

However, there will be times when tensions and issues arise. Codependency could not be avoided unless you acknowledge the symptoms and always be **aware of yourself.**

Self-awareness is key if you would like to avoid codependency in your future or present relationship. It is important to take a step back, take a breath, and reconsider what is happening to your relationship.

How To Avoid Becoming Codependent

Look at yourself. Evaluate. Do you have addictive tendencies? Have you had experiences of substance abuse, or are you currently abusing one?

Before you enter a relationship, make sure that you are in your **best form** and is emotionally and mentally ready for a relationship.

Always remember that relationships are not like the movies or novels where it is all about the feeling. Relationships in real life take work, effort, and partnership in order to succeed.

This is always a product of mutual investment by two people. If you do not know what real love is, or is currently having personal problems in your life, how can you successfully be in a relationship?

The best way to avoid a codependent relationship is to make sure that you are a healthy, self-sufficient individual before you enter one.

Be in a relationship not because you **need** it; be there because it is for the betterment of your character and individuality.

You should remember that codependency starts from needs that turn into addiction.

Always ask yourself: What does this relationship mean to me? What am I getting out of it?

Always be aware if you are "giving too much" or "needing" too much from the relationship. Feelings of love and acceptance are very beautiful, satisfactory feelings, but anything in excess is harmful.

This can always lead to addiction. These feelings can even serve as a blindfold when your relationship starts to take the abusive turn.

How To Evaluate Your Relationships

Satisfying relationships can only be described by one word: **satisfactory**. A good relationship should be good enough for you to stay in and invest your feelings in consciously. It should complement you as a person and make you feel whole.

There is no such thing as a "perfect" relationship. There will always be differences and disagreements between two persons.

You two may feel as if you have a perfect union or chemistry, but relationships are a completely different matter. There will always be compromise and imperfections in a relationship.

You would need to establish **healthy bounds** between the two of you in order to avoid codependency, which will ruin the relationship and make it abusive.

Are you over-praising your relationship? A sign that you are starting to become codependent is when you describe everything as overly perfect even when there are cracks and gaps in the relationship.

A healthy relationship is one that has bounds set (such as privacy and so on) as well as a shared aspect between two people.

Each of you needs to grow as individuals of your own. If you feel as if your world is revolving around the relationship, then you should take a step back and reevaluate.

Be honest to yourself: Do you have a life outside the relationship? If this relationship didn't exist in your life, where would you be now?

If you can't answer this question, this means that you have become codependent or are starting to become codependent.

You need to set bounds as early as possible to avoid further addiction to the relationship.

How To Set Bounds And Keep Everything Normal

If your relationship is fairly new, it is normal to wish that you could be with this person in every single day and in every single moment.

This is the honeymoon phase of the relationship.

However, as time passes, you should learn to set boundaries that, when crossed, signals that one person or the other is becoming **too demanding** or **abusive** in the relationship.

It is important to talk about what the two of you want or don't want in the relationship. Be vocal about this.

It might seem as if this is unnecessary since you are "perfectly in sync" and in love with each other, but you should understand that this is the best way to avoid abuse and codependency in the relationship. Learn to talk as two mature persons who respect one another.

What would you consider hurtful? When does giving and asking for attention become stressful for the two of you?

Discuss these matters and respect the compromise and the solution that you would come up. No matter what happens, always put respect each other.

More importantly, **have self-respect.** Codependency and abuse in relationships usually occur because people let abuse happen to them.

How To Address The Potential Break-Out Of Codependency

Does your partner keep on crossing the boundaries that you two have set? Do they always commit mistakes and end up apologizing to you?

On the other side, does your partner tolerate your ill-character and does not feel upset when you cross the boundaries of the relationship? Does your partner allow you to lose self-respect and sacrifice your own happiness and well-being, yet still encourage you to be in the relationship?

It is difficult to accept the fact that things can turn wrong in a relationship. Sometimes, a relationship is just not designed to work.

If mistakes have been repeatedly occurring and you keep making amends, but nothing turns out right in the end, you should address the situation before you become addicted to the cycle.

If you are feeling miserable but tell yourself that you **still love** being in the relationship, you are at risk of becoming codependent.

Talk to your partner and threaten to leave if the situation does not improve.

This may be very difficult for you, but you can always reclaim yourself after the break up.

If you do not see each other maturing as individuals, and if the relationship seems like a prison that hinders the growth of the two of you, then the best option is to **leave** or **take a break** before one of you starts to become codependent.

Do not fall in love with abusive relationships. It will never turn out right in the end. Your happiness and your well-being is your responsibility.

Chapter 10: Ropes That Hurt

Emotional dependence can become a real problem. When life revolves exclusively around another person, when there is no longer a space of its own, it is time to consider breaking the chains.

We understand codependency as a love that hurts. What irony, right? Something as beautiful as loving someone can suddenly become an ordeal.

This happens when we tie a person in a way we shouldn't. When we have not yet become aware that nobody belongs to us, but since childhood, we are taught that there is a kind of "property." Now I am yours, and you are mine, and vice versa. This is something we must start to change.

When love hurts

In all relationships between two people, conflicts will always arise. This is something natural, until it goes too far. When our partner begins to be the center of our all, when we develop codependency, since without it, we cannot manage to live our lives healthily, then we face a real problem.

That two people decide to share their life, love, respect, and live together, does not imply that they should depend on each other. Of course, they must continue respecting their spaces, and if the relationship does not work at any given time, nothing happens!

Our life cannot depend on anyone, it is only ours, and putting it in the hands of another person is almost like suicide. Therefore, you must consider what characterizes codependent people:

Your self-esteem always depends on what your partner can or cannot tell you.

You assume responsibilities that go far beyond your own, to try to meet the needs of your partner.

There is an absence of boundaries between the self and the other in the relationship.

You do not oppose your partner for fear of rejection.

When a relationship ends, it is immediately immersed in another.

If you have identified with some of these characteristics, you have probably suffered or been close to suffering from emotional dependence.

Release the ropes that imprison you

Do you know what it's like when you are grabbing a rope so that it does not slip from your hands? If, as soon as you release it, the rope escapes from your hands, the effort you are making right now will probably damage your hands!

The same is happening in your head in a situation of codependency. You are tying someone to a relationship that is not doing you any good. We are not going to say that it does not cost to release the rope, but sometimes we are somewhat masochistic, and we prefer to endure the atrocious pain that we are going through.

If you hesitate to release the rope, or if you are clear that it would be best to release it, but you do not see yourself capable or find it complicated, it is a good time to do it once and for all.

But ... does this make you happy? It should be an unusual situation, but you're not satisfied—it hurts. You cannot continue to let this wilt you; you must free yourself from those ropes. Only you are holding that suffering; nobody is forcing you except yourself.

Take the helm of your life

Once you make the decision, the liberation you will feel cannot even describe it. You will be filled with inner peace. It is clear that right now, you are afraid, insecure, your self-esteem shines because of your absence, and your confidence lies in that person who has the highest respect.

Of course, it is difficult to take the step, so if you do not see yourself trained for it, seek help. Without it, you may not have the courage to face all this alone.

At this point, it is convenient to review and ask yourself what has led you to this. Is there a problem in my past that could have caused this fear of losing someone? Does love surpass me?

Sometimes love is like a drug. It is reasonable to think of that person, to feel desires to be with her at all times... Emotional dependence causes you to get down, to humble yourself if necessary, to get him to continue with you.

And if he leaves you? You immediately look for a substitute or replacement. This is a severe problem; you don't know how to be alone! You need that drug that makes you feel good, even if you have to crawl if necessary.

Seek help, speak it, open your eyes to reality. It will cost, you will get it, you will suffer (but were you not already suffering?). You will pass the withdrawal syndrome, and it will be just you again.

Learn to be alone, reconcile yourself with loneliness. He doesn't have to make you feel insecure and lonely in this world. You are your best company.

Why we don't have the partner we want

Many times, the partner we want does not resemble anything we have. Is it because of nonconformity, not knowing how to choose or looking for the negative things?

We cannot always have the partner we want, and that is due to many reasons. However, we have the possibility of being happy with the other person and especially with ourselves. Keep reading this chapter to learn more.

How is the partner we want?

First of all it is very important to take the time to think a little and reflect on what we like and what we don't, about a partner. Surely you have the ability to realize what makes you feel good and what bothers you or hurts you.

In this way, it will be easier, if you look for a relationship, to find someone who meets or even exceeds expectations. But be careful, because many times we believe that to fall in love we must meet the ideal person, the prince of the stories or the heroines of the comics and we end up alone for a long time.

Knowing what we want is perfect, but being realistic will help us find love without much pretense. That does not mean that we do not value ourselves or anything like that, but that the man or woman without defects does not exist, or only appear in novels and movies.

We cannot give you a recipe or a magic solution; you and no one but you have the ability to determine what you want in this life. It is essential to set aside myths; the 'half orange' is not realistic, because nobody arrives to fill in what we need (or at least it shouldn't be like that).

Why don't we have the partner we want?

Believe it or not, we all have the person we want next to us. Or that at least we wanted at some point and it seemed to us that nobody could match him or beat him. But, with the passage of time we realized how things really are and that what seemed to be beautiful and eternal is not so much anymore.

And that's when the problems begin, the fights, the recriminations and the separations. Maybe we don't have the partner we want because we fear asking him to change what makes us suffer. Or because we don't dare to follow our path alone.

Worst of all, we endure and let time pass, until one day we realize that we have spent our lives with someone who really did not make us happy.

On the other hand, it is very important to keep in mind that if we are not satisfied with our relationship, it may not be due to the relationship itself, but to how we are.

This means that if we have placed all our expectations on the other person, if we have believed the fairy tale and think that only that person is able to make us feel good, then we are likely to get frustrated, angry and distressed.

Also, if you are not satisfied with yourself, it is almost impossible for you to be satisfied with those around you; and that includes a partner but also friends, family, work colleagues, etc.

And of course, we cannot ignore the constant pressure that the family or society puts on us. It is mandatory to be happy, to have the perfect partner and to comply with all cultural commandments.

Why do we want something different in a partner?

People are dissatisfied by nature and that has something good if we know how to handle it. Otherwise, we suffer too much ... and it's not worth it.

When we are alone we want to find someone to do certain activities with, but when we have a partner the most we do is go to the movies, dinner or the beach on a weekend. We loved that this person we met was so independent , but then it bothers us that he goes out with his friends so much.

We were happy to share our love of series and movies. But now, we get bored that this is the only plan of the weekend ... We could give thousands of other examples.

It is said that people want what they do not have instead of enjoying what they do have. It may seem difficult to understand, but it is simpler than you think.

We miss what we don't have for a dose of anxiety and 'futurism' that we don't know how to control. And instead, we should take a break, look around and be thankful for everything we have, including someone to love.

Chapter 11: Narcissist As Acodependency Magnate

It is said that narcissism and codependency are like two sides of the same coin. Not surprisingly narcissists and codependents seem to be attracted to each other like moths to a flame.

Narcissists can be very manipulative and controlling and when the codependent realizes what is happening, they may feel trapped and unable to get out. As a codependent it is important to be able to recognize a narcissist or narcissistic traits. This will help as you begin the journey to healing to avoid them if it all possible, or at least know how to deal with them appropriately.

First, what is a narcissistic personality disorder? This word has become common place in our vocabulary and with good reason. Social media seems to parade this type of behavior to an extreme. Of course, people with these tendencies are going to flock to places where they can be seen and admired, either online or offline.

The narcissist is associated with 'a grandiose sense of self-importance, a need for excessive admiration, and a lack of empathy' (DSM-5). Narcissists tend to be very self-centered and are in love with an idealized version of themselves. They are in love with this image because it allows them to avoid shortcomings in themselves, they don't want to acknowledge such as extreme insecurity.

Signs and Symptoms of NPD

Unlike codependency, Narcissistic Personality Disorder (NPD) is classified as a disorder in the Diagnostic Statistical Manual of Mental Disorder (DSM-5).

There are criteria that need to be met in order to make the definitive diagnosis.

Grandiose sense of self-importance - This is the defining characteristic of narcissism. It is a feeling of being special and somehow singled out for greatness. Narcissists are too good for just average money, relationships, lifestyle, etc. It doesn't matter that they haven't actually done anything to earn this status, they believe they should be seen as extraordinary anyway.

Have fantasies of power, success, intelligence, attractiveness etc. - These fantasies are supported by fabricated stories extolling their wonderfulness and intellect. The reality is they are hiding the inner emptiness they have and will not tolerate anything that doesn't support this inflated image of their accomplishments, attractiveness, etc. If they are challenged it will be met with rage or coldness.

Needing continual admiration - Like a never filling cup, the narcissist's incessant need for attention and admiration knows no bounds. The narcissist will surround himself with 'yes' men and the codependent is more than ready to serve in that role.

Sense of entitlement - The narcissist expects preferential treatment and deference from others. Will exploit others without guilt or shame - Narcissist have never developed the ability to walk in someone else's shoes. They lack empathy in other words. People are not individuals to them; they are tools to be used for their own gain.

A sense of Entitlement - Special people should be treated special. They've earned it in their eyes and expect it. How have they earned it? Just by being wonderful of course, or smart, or attractive. Doesn't matter really. Unwilling or unable to empathize with the feelings of others.

Pompous and arrogant behavior. It's pretty easy to see that if you put a narcissist based on the above characteristics with a codependent, we have the making of something that can only end in disaster if it isn't caught and or dealt with.

Ann Brown writes about how the narcissist will use certain tactics and strategies to shame the codependent into complying with their wishes.

Shame - Both the codependent and narcissist share the same goal of hiding shame. It forces both to hold onto dysfunctional behaviors.

Magical Thinking - Or the belief that one's thoughts can influence the world. The codependent will build up the narcissist. He or she is doing this in order to convince themselves (the codependent) that they really are with a great person. Both are working to keep this type of thinking alive.

Arrogance-The codependent will accept the ridicule and pretend it isn't happening. They become numb to the abuse. Numbness is a very important tool in the codependent's arsenal.

Envy - The codependent is so beat down that their self-esteem could not possibly see how the narcissist could be envious of anything. Therefore, the put downs and minimization of accomplishments is not viewed as envy.

Entitlement - As a codependent it is part of their behavior to flatter and aggrandize everything for the narcissist. This feeds into the narcissist's need for validation and praise, thus completing the cycle for the codependent who lives for praising others.

Exploitation - By ignoring the abuse or being taken advantage of, because the focus is on being liked, the codependent overlooks the exploitation. If pointed out the ability to rationalize, a core codependent skill, comes into play. The exploitation can be financial, emotional, physical, or spiritual. However, it manifests itself, the codependent will do everything to overlook it.

Bad Boundaries - make it very difficult to build self-esteem and confidence. The focus would be taken off of pleasing people and ignoring abuse. With bad boundaries the codependent sees it as their job to make sure their narcissistic partner's needs come firs Chapter 4   So, Are You Codependent?

Addiction to Food in Co-dependency

Food enablers are the co-dependent factors of increasing or adding to one's obesity or overeating disorders. Co-dependent partners that can add to one's eating disorders can be the parent, the kids, the partners or the friends. Due to the aforementioned harmful effects of co-dependency, some of the emotional imbalances of anxiety, restless, hypersensitivity, depression and stress can add to venting out the same through over-eating.

Spouses of the food-a-holics will try to please their partners by cooking exotic delicacies that render the subject and the partner to become obese on their own. Even though the co-dependent tries to limit the food intake of the partner and put down rules of healthy food diets, the love and other factors of co-dependent makes them the food enablers that lead to the obesity of both, in the due time. One's lack of communication and other misunderstanding inclusive of the intimacy issues can pull the reasons for venting out the aspects of anxiety through eating. Co-dependents should instead show the delight of delicacy through healthy diet.

Another theory of psychology dictates that co-dependency itself arises from a family dysfunction of overeating or obesity. When someone in a family has the habit of overeating, the children and other family members are also invited to the sumptuous dining, every time the food

116

addict has a rush or pang, hence inducing the same overeating disorder in the rest of the family. This also teaches the family that overeating is a pleasant vent out or resolution for one's anxieties depression and stress.

Workaholics as part of co-dependency Parameter

Do you feel that the undue business tours and official appointments of our partner is leaving you lonely, unsatisfied, compromised and confined without any bliss in your relationship? Then your co-dependency is largely dependent on your partner's workaholic nature.

Workaholism is one of the biggest cause and effects of maintaining stability in a family, A workaholic patriarchal or simply, the head in a family enables the rest of the family to feel incomplete and discontent with the time spent with the workaholic. This induces a dissatisfactory co-dependence on account of the subject. They tend to adjust, compromise and fake affection to mask the absence and dissatisfaction with the concerned workaholic. Gradually, the rest of the family grown into a dysfunction of perspective that work is the only duty one should regard and respect. This instils a sense of detachment with morals, humanity, warmth and family values as each individual member of the family grows to regard their work of utmost importance.

Exemplifying, a highly workaholic businessperson father or mother can instill in their kids a sense of loneliness, detachment and ideology that is centered on the belief of delivering just productivity, money and profit as the morals of their life. The kid learns to regard his work more than his own family, and hence run to work even at his girl's deathbed.

t and foremost. It leads to an almost arrogance about how 'good I am' at dealing with difficult people.

Chapter 12: Moving On From A Codependent Relationship

In some instances, a person must simply get out of a codependent relationship. Whether it's due to physical abuse (which no person should ever be subjected to, period), one party's unwillingness to change, or simply because you've had enough and no longer even wish to be in the relationship any longer, you may find yourself in the situation of having to leave a codependent relationship.

Usually it's fear that keeps a person in an unhealthy relationship. Either you're fearful of being alone or feel obligated to stay in order to maintain your partner's happiness; either way, these are not healthy reasons for staying with someone.

Staying in a codependent relationship that's unfixable for whatever reason is an almost certain way to sabotage your mental, or even physical, wellbeing. Perhaps the codependency has gone so far that it's reached the point at which you feel comfortable experiencing constant emotional pain. If that's the case, and you've concluded that the relationship is past the point of improvement, you must get out.

Unfortunately, people are typically pushed to their breaking points before they can recognize the fact that they must get out of the relationship. Typically, a partner's actions lead to the codependent experiencing a sense of anger. You've been hurt in a way that you didn't think was possible, or perhaps you've been fed up for far too long. Most likely, this awakening will come in the form of anger.

What you have to do, then, is recognize this anger. Although it's a negative emotion, it will fuel your ability to reclaim your self-worth after you've constantly given so much of yourself away for so long.

Because codependency generally stems from a lack of establishing boundaries, it's essential to hone in on this sense of anger. Here's why: anger instinctually encourages you to raise your boundaries. Your natural defense is to reestablish your sense of self, by realizing that you are a person with valid feelings and thoughts that have been disregarded.

Of course, recognizing your anger does not mean that you should act irrationally, violently, or cruelly. It's simply a means of recognizing the fact that you must preserve your wellbeing and livelihood.

Ending a relationship is almost always difficult. Especially for codependents, it requires a great deal of strength and courage, as well as resolve. Here are some things to keep in mind when ending a codependent relationship:

Don't just lay all the blame on one party. You don't have to take any blame, either, but remember that pointing fingers at this point in your relationship is senseless. Unfortunately, the truth is that codependency is created by a combination of both parties' behaviors.

Be direct about why you're leaving. Tell the other individual how and why you feel that you've been wronged.

Don't seek revenge, or purposely try to hurt the other person. Regardless of how hurt you may be feeling, it will only cause you both to feel more pain if you try to be destructive at the end of your relationship. Once you've left the relationship, you'll need to reestablish your own living space. Whether you get a place of your own or your partner leaves, make your living space individualistic by decorating and arranging things the way you see fit.

Following that, you must reclaim your own sense of self-worth. Rediscover the hobbies or activities that you once enjoyed, or seek new ones. Spend time with family and friends, but make sure to set aside some time just for you.

While you may be a bit fragile when you first leave a codependent relationship, keep in mind that things will only improve as time goes on. You'll become stronger and more independent. In order to do so, however, you must be willing to change a bit on your own, as well.

For one thing, try to banish negativity by remembering to be kind to yourself. Don't judge yourself so harshly, and instead, praise yourself for all of the goals (however small they may seem) that you've accomplished.

Also, try to be welcoming when it comes to accepting help from others. Seek strong, caring individuals who genuinely want to see you succeed and support your goal of fostering healthy relationships.

Finally, if and when you find yourself ready to move on and seek a new relationship, truly take the time to assess your feelings. Don't settle just out of fear of being alone - before looking for a partner, think about what your needs are in a relationship. What qualities do you look for in a partner? How can you make sure that your needs are met? Remind yourself that you deserve love and happiness, but keep in mind that you, first and foremost, are responsible for your own happiness. Create happiness, self-worth, and self-love, and then you can move on to create a loving relationship with another.

Chapter 13: Exercises

So now you have set boundaries for yourself and for your everyday life, how, specifically can you develop healthy boundaries in your relationship?

These exercises should be attempted in a calm, neutral space. You should try to work through these exercises in a relaxed state of mind. Attempting them when you are frustrated and upset will simply lead you to linger on the negatives and foisting the responsibility on to the actions of others.

When you are setting your boundaries do not feel ashamed or guilty when setting them. If you experience negative feedback from these new boundaries do not give up, people around you may feel angry simply because they cannot manipulate you they way they have been used to. It is important to maintain your sense of purpose and individuality. Those who truly care for you will support your attempts to take control of your own happiness.

You too must respect your own boundaries. If you decided, for example, that you will not accept any extra work from you co-workers you must enforce this. You must respect your boundaries or others will not either.

It is difficult to remain strong and enforce these boundaries. Begin by simply exploring your own feelings. Truly identify what it is that makes you happy and abandon the guilt that others may pile onto you in an attempt for you to forgo your own needs and pander to their own. Remember people are not necessarily against you, they are simply out for themselves.

Once you form a boundary you will find that it is easier to pursue the things that you enjoy. You will find that, although it is difficult to enforce in the beginning, maintaining the boundary will be easier with time as you begin to reap the rewards. The immense amount of time and energy that you expended on maintaining another person or craving their acceptance will suddenly free up, giving you time to pursue your own interests.

To help you get into the right mindset and to start setting your boundaries we have included a few exercises to help you reduce your stress. These were pioneered by Dr Herbert Benson at Harvard and will help you ease your anxiety and anger to enable you to serenely analysis your own feelings.

Find a space that is open and de-cluttered.

Sit in a position where you can be comfortable and restful.

Close your eyes to any external distractions.

Relax your muscles. Start with your toes and move upwards. Either aloud or silently say to yourself each body part as you relax it. Move up through your body and finish with your head.

Breathe freely and count your breaths. Think only about inhaling and exhaling.

Do this for ten minutes.

Do not get up immediately but open your eyes and contemplate why you are attempting to build these boundaries in a constructive and objective way.

This is easy to do on your own but in the real world; of course there will be many distractions. You must remember, however, to keep the focus on yourself and not relapse into thinking about the other person's reaction or needs.

If you find yourself watching or analyzing your partner's movements or words too closely take a step back. Try not to think about their actions in relation to anything you've done. Instead of trying to guess what each little gestures means try to start a calm dialogue to ask them how they are feeling.

Try not to place your partner on a pedestal. Are your expectations of behavior realistic? Try not to think about expectations you have for others, but rather are you fulfilling the expectations you have set for yourself?

Remember you are not the sole cause of everything that is happening around you. People are influenced by many things, their own thoughts, feelings and other people. Take responsibility for your actions alone.

It is important to have your own interests and hobbies. By building your sense of self you will gain confidence in your own ability. Encourage your partner to do the same. As you both grow you will have more to share and enjoy together.

By creating a stress free environment to analysis your true goals and motivations you can begin to build the foundations on which you can grow your own self-esteem. By stopping and critically analyzing common situations you find yourself in, with your own happiness as the primary motive, you will be able to find your own independence and respect.

Chapter 14: Get Professional Help Or Counselling.

You should really consider seeking professional help or counselling. This can help you in choosing a path that will benefit you and your loved one towards achieving a better quality of life than you are presently living. They can help you to stop being an enabler to your addicted loved one. You must come to terms with the fact that by being an enabler you are contributing to your loved one staying an addict. You may be thinking that you don't give them drugs or supply them; perhaps not directly but indirectly you do. When you do things like give them money when you know that they are going to more than likely spend the money on whatever they are addicted to, you're contributing to their addiction. Whether it is gambling, drugs, or alcohol whatever their addiction is you know in your heart that they will spend any money or most of it on their drug of choice.

On this note, I want to mention that I am a Co-Active Professional Certified Coach and specialize in working with people who have loved ones addicted to substances. I work with them to continue moving forward with their life so that they can still enjoy it, despite the loved ones' addiction difficulties. For more information, take a look at my website,

How to Love an Addict and Stay Healthy

Eating the proper foods or diet is one of the best medicines you can offer your body. If you are eating a healthy diet it will help to keep you strong both mentally and physically in order to deal with the everyday stresses resting on your shoulders. It is not going to do you or your loved one any good if you fall into ill health due to a poor diet and lack of exercise.

In order for you to keep up your strength you must put the focus from the addict you love to yourself and start showing some self-love in doing things to improve your health and happiness. Don't spend all your time obsessing about when or how your loved one is going to seek help for their addiction because the hard reality is they may never choose to seek help.

You don't have to give up loving the addict in your life but you must start loving yourself enough to take care of your personal wants and needs.

Preparing Healthier Meals

Start making changes by getting yourself and loved one on a healthy diet plan. Stop buying any junk foods but instead try and eat as much organic or fresh produce as you can. Perhaps you could follow a certain weekly diet routine having all your daily meals planned out. Let the addicted person know that you are going to prepare healthy meals from now on for you both.

Make sure to have a weekly list for the foods you will need for your meals that week and try to stick with what is on the list. Remember this when you are shopping: if it is not on the list then you do not need it. If your addicted loved one tries to complain about the food choices and wants you to get junk food stay firm and say no. Let them understand that you are only going to be getting the foods for your healthy meals and nothing more.

You must make sure to explain to the addict in your life that you are making some changes in lifestyle that will help improve your health. You will only be making the meals that are included in your diet plan; you will not be buying and making them extra food but they will be eating the healthy meals too. This is a way you can help both of you in that you prepare both of your meals so you can decide on choosing healthy choices in meals when you do your meal planning.

You may not be able to get your addicted loved one to give up their addiction but you can be in control of the types of meals you are serving them.

Getting Exercise

Once you have your healthy meal plan set up you should start thinking about doing some form of physical exercise to help keep you in shape. It is so important to make sure that you are getting regular exercise to help to keep you in good health. Your loved one may not be interested in getting exercise because their addiction is running their lives, causing them to have no energy or interest in anything but getting their next fix. You must not let this deter you from seeking exercise for yourself because you must look after your own health and well-being.

Perhaps you could join a local gym. This could give you a chance to get out of the house and meet new people who will be a positive influence in your life. You may find you really enjoy going to the gym and working-out. Don't let the addict in your life try and talk you out of going to the gym. Stay strong and keep doing it for yourself and your much deserved happiness. Don't let them bring you down by their negative comments. Even if you make a point to go for a 30 minute walk after dinner each evening this would also be a great way to get out and get some exercise.

Don't Give in

Do not stop looking after yourself because the addict in your life is trying to manipulate you and all your time in tending to their wants and needs. They may try to get you to stop with the healthy diet and exercise because they don't want to lose you. They may have a fear that you will get healthy and in shape and realize one day that you no longer want to be with them. They don't want you to improve yourself for fear that you will continue to want better things in life such as a healthier and happier life shared with someone who is not an addict.

They Don't Care About Your Needs

They are frightened that you will meet new and better people when you are out and about and this is the last thing they want. They want to keep you down and out right at their side tending to all of their wants and needs not tending to any of your own needs. They are not thinking of what is good for you as addicts tend to be selfish only thinking of themselves and ways they can manipulate those around them to do their bidding.

By continuing to put you down, they want you to feel that no one else would be interested in being involved with you; they make you feel like they are doing you a favour by letting you be a part of their life. They don't want you to build your self-confidence up and instead they want you to believe that you are nothing without them in your life. Addicts are great at making those around them feel that they are in some way lucky that they are part of the addicts' life. They make sure your self-esteem is not real good so they are able to use that in manipulating you to do what they ask of you without resistance. They try and keep control of your life by keeping you feeling down and hopeless about yourself making you feel worthless. These are tactics they will use in order to keep control of you and get you to continue to enable their addiction.

Stop Blaming the Addict for Everything

You must stand up and face the music and be ready to claim your part in contributing to your loved one's addiction. You must also acknowledge that all the bad things that went wrong in your life were not all the addicted loved ones fault. Part of your healing process is being able to stand up and face your responsibilities and accepting some of the blame and not putting it all on to the addicted loved one. The sooner you come to terms with the fact that you were an enabler of your loved one's addiction the quicker the road will be towards finding inner peace with yourself for the wrongs you have done in your life. You cannot blame someone else for how things worked out in your life; you are the one responsible for your own actions, not anyone else. We all make mistakes in life as none of us are perfect, but we have to lay claim to them in order to move forward in life in a peaceful manner. It is always easier to blame someone else such as the addict in your life for all the things that didn't go right for you.

Taking a Close Look at Why You are an Enabler

To help with your personal healing process you must confront the reasons why you have continued to be an enabler for your addicted loved one. Was it just easier for you to give in and give them whatever they wanted? Perhaps by keeping yourself busy in dealing with the addict in your life and their issues it was helping you to avoid confronting your own issues. One of those being that you are being co-dependent or acting as an enabler. It is not going to be easy coming to terms with the reality of the situation you are in. Just remember that Rome wasn't built in a day and neither will your new way of living a more productive and healthier life. It is going to take commitment on your part as well as inner strength. You are going to have to draw deep within yourself to find the strength to continue towards a healthier happy way of living.

You should think about seeking professional help to find out why you have made the choices you have to this point in your life. Sometimes it can be a great advantage to get a third party's view on your life and why you are living the way you are at this point. Sometimes we can't see the trees in the forest so it helps to have others give us advice and support in trying to make better choices in our life. They can help you to find ways to break the bad cycle of making bad choices time and time again. You must take control and be responsible for your own actions -this is an important stepping stone towards finding inner peace.

Chapter 15: Consequences Of A Codependent Relationship

While a codependent relationship may sometimes seem like a good thing, long term, feelings of unexpressed emotions and hurt feelings usually develop. Since these relationships tend to be very one-sided, eventually, the person who is continually being used is bound to start feeling resentment toward their counterpart.

These types of relationships are often unsustainable long term, yet for some reason, they perpetuate just the same. Plenty of people are miserable and suffer through codependent relationships for the sake of familiarity. It is easier to stay in their current relationship than it is to break the emotional and logistical bonds that hold them together. When it comes to spouses, this means divorce, splitting up assets and dealing with the fallout of the relationship. Unless something is truly unbearable, living a mediocre life like this seems better than the alternative.

Due to the increased stress felt during times of resentment, the physical and emotional bodies both suffer. The consequences of unhealthy, unfulfilling relationships are scientifically proven. As stress builds, the body's immune system becomes overworked to the point of exhaustion. Stress causes sleep disruption and energy becomes hard to come by. You just can't be yourself if your body and mind are exhausted. Just as when you are tired, your immune system gets sloppy and begins to defend the body against things it normally wouldn't/ Sometimes that even means it attacks body tissues. Weight gain can occur as well as a host of autoimmune diseases can develop like rheumatoid arthritis, lupus, celiac disease and much more. Part of taking care of your body as a whole is taking care of your emotional health and spirit, and being in a highly demanding relationship is part of that.

Besides your personal health, the well-being of those around you begins to suffer as well. Other members of your family or friends may feel as they are being cast aside because all of your time is focused on one relationship. You may act a bit irritable or withdrawn toward others, as your stress levels increase. Children or roommates often suffer as well, especially if the relationship spirals into arguing and yelling. Whether done in private or not, it is hard to ignore the tension that builds, and it becomes palpable to those around you.

Long term, dysfunctional relationships inhibit you from being who you are supposed to be. Whether you feel you are being used or are the defined user, your life is impacted by this relationship. If you are being used, a good majority of your time and energy will be invested in this other person. Go ahead and think about how much time you spend daily on relationships that really give you nothing in return. What could you be doing with that time instead? You may have considered furthering your career, meeting new friends, trying new activities, yet this relationship has kept you pinned to your usual routine. Feeling guilty about going out and trying new things is a hindrance on your life, and it's about time you lived the life you were meant to live instead of settling in for the dysfunction.

If you have defined yourself as the user in this relationship, think about the person you often use. Since you are not reciprocating the generosity they have shown you, think of all of the things they have given up to help you. How does it make you feel to know that you have kept someone you supposedly love from living their dreams?

Now go ahead and think about you. Think of all of the menial tasks you asked that person to carry out, things you could have done for yourself had you taken the time to learn something new. You could be a better person should you have tried harder, done more things on your own, grown as a person. Wouldn't you feel so much more accomplished if you had taken the initiative to do more for yourself? Now that you feel bad, take a few minutes to throw yourself a pity party, then get to work.

The lesson here is that even though you may feel the immediate benefits of codependency, the good feeling of helping someone else, or having a friend help you, the long term consequences to a one-sided codependent relationship are detrimental for both parties. If your original goal was to ultimately help someone else, it is important to realize now that you may be hindering their progress. It is important to help friends and family members when they need help, and it is certainly okay to ask for help when you truly need it. If you do need help, make sure you have thought your problem through and exhausted all options before taking the easy way out. If you are on the giving end of this problem, help your friend or family member by working through the problem with them, not just giving them the answer.

We have all heard the phrase, "Give a man a fish, he will eat for a day. Teach a man to fish, and he will never go hungry. It is much more important to teach than to give, and it is also important to set boundaries and protect your best interests as well. This may sound a bit callous, but if you consider that overhelping somebody will only hold them back, in the long run, it makes it easier to take a step back in the moment.

We must also discuss the case of the sick family member again. In this case, there really isn't much manipulation coming from the sick party. This person may have cancer, going through treatment, and they physically can't do things for themselves. They are not asking for help with something because they don't feel like it, they are literally incapable. Often, their caretakers take pride in the fact that they are keeping their family members going through a trying experience. However, a great amount of time and energy is often put in to make that happen. Per the definition, these caregivers often forego other parts of their lives to take care of others.

A long term sickness, like dementia in an elderly parent, can require attention from the child for years on end. When those parents pass, the children often report not knowing what to do. They may have spent every waking moment with the parent, caring for their every need, and suddenly, nobody needs them anymore. They have no idea what to do with their free time, even drawing a blank on what they used to do for fun. While they eventually recover, this shows just how separated a person can become from their normal life when they are engrossed in a codependent relationship. While caring for a sick friend or family member is admirable, it is important to draw boundaries, even though it may feel selfish to do so. Ask for help in caring for the person, either from other family members or friends, or seek professional services that will take some of the burdens off of you. Remember that it is not selfish, you must care for yourself and be healthy before you have any capability of taking care of others.

Chapter 16: Regaining Your Independence

To get you started on your journey towards recovery here are our top tips for helpful exercises that you can begin at home. We have focused on the three biggest causes of co-dependence; unbalanced relationships, guilt and self-esteem.

These three topics are essential to all of our own happiness, and they are areas that you should look to work on throughout the process of recovery and beyond. Before you tackle the Big Three however, here are some first steps you can take to set you on your own journey and prepare you to tackle the big issues.

First Steps

First you must regain your center of control. Look deeply into your actions and think about your motives. Did you undertake these actions for you own benefit, or were you acting because of or on behalf of someone else's needs? When we are used to doing things and stuck in certain routines it is easy to forget why it is we're doing them. Take a step back and consider your motivations.

In any recovery from addiction abstinence is an important feature. You must detangle yourself from the feelings of those around you. Learn to distinguish when you're doing an action for you own benefit rather than from a need to receive approval. Evaluate clearly your own values and try not to perform any action which violates your own beliefs.

When you find yourself thinking about another's actions, instead of fretting about it, remember that people react and act according to numerous factors. It is unlikely that you are the cause of all their actions. If you truly believe that you are the cause of their behavior then simply learn to ask, in a neutral way, whether your actions have affected that person and listen to their answer.

Second you must be aware of your own needs and act on them. Codependents are notorious for sacrificing their own values and goals on the altar of their partner's happiness. If you have naturally nurturing instincts it is hard to restrict yourself from trying to help others. However, by doing so you are denying yourself and interfering where your help may not be necessary, or even enabling bad behavior to continue.

You may not even realize that you are ignoring your own needs. Try to allocate yourself times during the week where you do something purely for yourself. By learning to pursue activities that make you happy, as you reap the rewards you will find it easier to deny unwarranted demands upon your time. This is tied in very tightly with raising your self-esteem, which we will explore later.

All of these actions require sufferers to admit that their symptoms go beyond the normal codependent behaviors we exhibit. You may say to yourself, well everyone behaves this way sometimes, or, well I just don't have time for myself, that's life! Instead of comparing yourself to symptoms or to other people, simply ask yourself if you are you happy. Are these behaviors causing you to feel depressed or restricted? Are they impacting your life?

No matter how severe or unremarkable your symptoms are, if you can answer yes to the above questions, then you can acknowledge that you need to make some changes. Even if you find it too hard to admit that you might be suffering from codependency, at least admit that you want to make changes to your life for the better. This will let you take the first important step on the path to acceptance.

Acceptance is a vital step, but it is not just an acceptance of codependency. You must learn to accept yourself. It is learning to place a greater value on your own needs and taking them into account when making decisions. For example, if a relation asks for your help to organize a dinner party, ask yourself how detrimental it would be to you to accept. If you already have too much on your plate, you should politely decline rather that bowing to social pressure to join. Explain that you already have too many demands on your time and to sacrifice any more of your time will affect you detrimentally.

Once you have begun to look at your actions in this new light and accept that things need to change you must take action. Whilst you may now have a new awareness of your behaviors being inappropriate or detrimental to your situation, you must now take steps to correct this.

Stepping outside your comfort zone is difficult. You must begin to take an active role in discussions, instead of passively accepting tasks, question the merits of you undertaking it. Try to start allocating responsibility evenly between yourself and others at home and work. Help support your loved ones towards the goals rather than pursuing them on their behalf.

Most importantly you must follow through with your actions. You must abide by your own new assertiveness or else no one else will either. It is no point announcing to colleagues that you will no longer be taking more than your fair share of a project, whilst still doing the work.

Whilst stepping into the light to take these new actions you must remember not to aim for perfection. You will have set backs but you must not be disheartened, failure is a necessary repercussion of living. Remember that ships that remain in the harbor will be safe but they will never achieve anything. However, with negatives always come positives. By engaging in new activities you'll learn more about yourself and how you can enjoy the world.

Start to regain your control by accepting that you need to change and taking positive steps towards active improvement. These initial steps will be difficult at first, but as you notice changes for the better in your life you will be able to find more and more reasons to continue.

Whilst these first steps are crucial, you must also work on the core causes of codependency. Below we have included some helpful exercises and thinking points on how to improve your relationships, manage guilt and most crucially improve your self-esteem.

To get you started on your journey towards recovery here are our top tips for helpful exercises you can begin at home. We have focused on the three biggest causes of co-dependence; unbalanced relationships, guilt and self-esteem.

Regaining Inter-Dependence

Admittedly, inter-dependence sounds as foreboding and unhealthy as co-dependence, but this is codependency's opposite. To be in an inter-dependent relationship is to be in a partnership where you take care of both yourself and each other. It is all about keeping your relationship on an equilibrium where you can rely on your partner and equally they can rely on you. A balancing act is always one that is difficult and entails constant adjustments that require clear communication from both parties

In order to achieve this we suggest that you explore the following questions:

Identify the positives in your relationship. What makes you happy? What do you want to continue doing? By focusing on the positives you can bring unity back into the relationship as you explore things you can enjoy together.

If there's something that doesn't make you happy why is that? Could you do something to improve this, or is it something you want to stop altogether? By communicating clearly and without pandering to each other's needs you can clearly explore the negative aspects of your relationship. By clearly identifying these issues it will be much easier to prevent them happening again.

It is important that you and your partner approach these questions from the same view point. When asking yourself the above questions are you both agreeing on what makes you happy? It's always ok to agree to disagree on things, no partnership agrees on everything, but it is important to have sufficient common ground in order to make a steady foundation for your future together.

What is it that you want from your partner right now? What do you think you will want in the future? Setting out your needs will establish what you expect from your partner and why you have felt distressed when these needs are not met. This will ensure clarity for the future, preventing partner's confusion when their significant other is upset, and hopefully preventing them from making the same mistake.

What is it that your partner wants from you? What does your partner want in the future? It is important of course to listen to your partner's needs as well. By ensuring you are both taking care of each other it will ensure that you will not fall back into the same patterns of becoming a care giver and an enfeebled recipient.

In this future do you both have a common goal to work towards? Working towards a future together will be a unifying and rewarding experience.

Finally, ask yourselves what you could do to improve yourselves individually? By being able to work on projects separate from your relationship you will be able to retain a stronger sense of self, ensuring that you do not become completely dependent on each other again. Instead of deteriorating together now you will be able to grow stronger together as an individual and a couple.

Over Coming Guilt

This section should be prefaced by saying that not all guilt is bad. Our guilt acts as an important moral counter weight and indictor to tell us when we are right and wrong.

However, being able to forgive ourselves is crucial to our self-esteem. This can be difficult as guilt often lingers on our consciousness well after the events that caused it. Despite that, it is imperative that you let this guilt go as it can be extremely detrimental to you and hinder your recovery.

Guilt often manifests itself with other negative emotions such as anger, not only with yourself but with others. Indeed you might even find that you feel guilt on behalf of others, a frequent characteristic of codependency.

If the guilt you are feeling is for actions you are culpable for them accept it, take responsibility for it. If you are able to make amends you should do so, accept that you have done all you can to make the situation right and feel free to move on with your life.

If you are finding it difficult to find the core reason for your guilt you may find it easier to write it down or talk about it aloud. By having to rationalize to another person or to write it down the root of the problem may become clear.

Ask yourself by whose standards you are judging yourself? Are the values your own or your parents, or maybe those of your faith? What do you gain by their approval? Is the benefit of their approval better than the ability to feel you own self-worth?

Do you still feel the same way about the event that caused the guilt? Do you hold the same values, would you act differently now? Be honest with yourself and examine your values closely. If you can see that you have grown since the event, you can comfort yourself by knowing that should you encounter the same situation again you would handle it better. If not, then you can identify a clear goal to work towards.

Finally, after examining your values, ask yourself whether your previous actions are in line with those values. Were those actions worth the hurt you caused yourself by going against your own values, whatever they may be? In the future when faced with difficult decisions, you can remember the negative outcome that resulted from abandoning your values, giving you the conviction to stick to them.

Building Self-Esteem

Your Inner Voice

It is easy for those around you to tell you that you need a greater self-esteem. It is easy for them to, at a wave of a hand; dismiss feelings of inadequacy as stupid and unwarranted. However, building your self-esteem is one of the biggest and most challenging tasks a human can attempt, especially in a world that is so often attempting to break it down.

We hope that the following guide will help you begin to build the foundations for a strong self-esteem that will remain unshaken by the world.

First, that little critical voice inside you head? You need to get it to simmer down. We all have the voice, whispering and criticizing our thoughts, comparing us unfavorably to our friends and colleagues.

But it can help spur us on as well. When it says to you that you're not good at something, think to yourself, how can I make myself better at it then? Be proactive about it; actively direct your thoughts away from the negative by engaging them in something. Read an article online on how to improve, book a course or read a book, your mind is now too busy to be shouting negatives at you.

Or if it's something that you can't change about yourself, come up with a little phrase to stop your train of thoughts. Shout 'Stop!' to yourself and re-focus your thoughts. Think about your plans for the weekend or a new recipe you want to try.

Motivate Yourself

To help keep that critical voice silent it might be helpful to write down your goals. When they're out on paper it will make them feel more realistic and attainable. Now write down all the amazing benefits you can get when you achieve your goal. Start with something simple at first, like saving for a holiday or making time to have dinner with your partner more often.

Do something you love

We rarely find it difficult to do something we love. If you are still struggling to motivate yourself to do something, ask yourself is that what you really want? Is there something better out there that I could focus on that would make me happy?

Don't be perfect

Being a perfectionist is seriously hard work. It's also impossible. Nothing is ever perfect and by setting off with perfection in mind you're almost certainly going to feel disappointed at the result, even if the results are still pretty amazing! This can also lead to crippling procrastination, by being afraid to fail before you even begin.

Just set off to do the best you can do. There will always be people who can do something better that you can but everyone has some unique ability that makes them different. Find yours.

Face Failure

It is a rare thing in this world to attempt something and succeed on the first try. Many successful writers and entrepreneurs were criticized and rejected on their first tries, (and some on their eleventh and twentieth goes!).

Failure it not something unique to you and trying something new almost always means a new learning process. Often it is the doing of something that gives us the most pleasure rather than finishing it anyway. Failure is simply a necessary and integral part of the learning curve.

If you try a job and find you don't like, or aren't good at it, just remind yourself you haven't failed, it just isn't the right thing for you.

Chapter 17: Getting Started In Recovery

While no two relationships are exactly the same, neither are codependent relationships. There is a great deal of diversity and variables within relationships, and at any given time, codependency can exist or not exist. This is why experts in the field of psychology have trouble identifying what exactly a codependent relationship is. What we do know is that people with certain personality types are prone to this type of relationship and that these habits are often learned early on, usually in childhood.

While it is possible for anybody to have healthy relationships, those who grew up with parents in healthy, well-adjusted relationships tend to have a leg up against those who were raised in a household constantly engrossed in emotional turmoil and disagreement. The idea of nature versus nurture says that the personality traits of a person are variable both by the genes of the person, but also the environment they grew up in. It would be hard to ignore the fact that a child would be affected by their environment, but also by genes from their parents.

While it may seem obvious that a child from a broken home would grow up and mimic the same habits, we must also consider the role that codependency between parent and child has on future relationships. Studies show that children who are coddled by their parents and who rely on the parents for everyday tasks will be attracted to a mate who will do the same for them.

If a parent consistently takes care of a child's every need, especially when doing things the child could easily do for themselves, they lack the confidence it takes to make it out on their own. This could be anything from cooking, cleaning, doing laundry, or even having the parents deal with conflicts between friends and classmates. When a parent plays too big of a role in their child's life, they actually teach them that they don't need to try, because someone will always be there to take care of them when times get tough. Unfortunately, as these children get older and begin looking for spouses, they look for someone they can depend on. While finding a mate you can rely on is a good trait, depending on them to do the things they can do themselves is selfish, and perpetuates the codependent relationship they had with the parent.

Another offshoot of this is with very strict parenting. Having a laundry list of rules to follow during childhood teaches discipline, but there is a fine line between learning life skills and becoming a prime candidate for a codependent relationship. Often times, if the rules are not followed, the parent can become angry or disappointed, and the child learns that they are doing well by the mood of the parents. The child can feel happy when they please their parents, and all self-worth is established through these means. The child's sole source of emotional well-being comes from the parents, and not from their own self-esteem. What they learn is that doing things right or wrong, in a very black and white way, is the basis of a good relationship. As they enter find spouses, they will carry out the same relationship. They become dependent on making their spouse happy, and if they don't their self-esteem diminishes. What perpetuates it even further is if their spouse depends on them to do simple tasks for them, making the relationship highly one-sided.

Certain personality traits are often seen in codependent relationships, and if you tend to relate to these traits, it may be time to take a closer look at your relationships. While it is not your destiny to be codependent, you may be more susceptible if you are a people pleaser. This type of person avoids conflict and will do whatever is necessary to avoid it. In childhood, these kids are often the teacher's favorite, never getting in trouble, as defying the rules would cause conflict and make their parents unhappy, the stem of their self-worth.

Further down the line, this person may fall victim to an emotionally of physically abusive relationship, as the burden of sticking up for themselves and ending a relationship would impose on their abuser. They would rather stay in the relationship than going through the conflict of ending it. Their self-esteem is so dependent on the wants and needs of their abuser, that leaving would cause inner turmoil as well, which is why so many people end up staying in these types of relationships.

People who are prone to depression or anxiety are also good candidates for codependency. Although the scientific community has not officially recognized codependency disorder as an official diagnosis, links are clear between mental disorders like anxiety and depression and codependency. This is likely because all three problems are usually caused by issues with self-esteem. When self-worth is defined by how you are perceived by others, it becomes difficult to cope with someone being unhappy with you. To remedy this, people often enter into codependent relationships in order to make them happy, or defying this lowers self-esteem, leading to anxiety and depression. Either way, it can be a very tough habit to break.

Codependency is also perpetual between generations. The environment you were raised in often dictates how you will raise your own children. The habits and parenting skills you were exposed to early on stick with you, and unless a valiant effort is made to teach your children a different way of life, you will likely end up parenting your kids the same way your parents raised you. In the case of a dysfunctional, codependent upbringing, this leaves little hope that your child will have a different life.

The good news is, once the habits you have developed can be recognized as dysfunctional or co-dependent, it becomes much easier to change those habits. You cannot stop what you don't recognize as a problem. Therefore, just by reading this book and recognizing that you may have some codependent habits, you can change that in yourself so that future generations will benefit from strong, healthy relationships with friends and loved ones.

Chapter 18: Basic Self Care For Codependency

After Julia's divorce, she took it upon herself to start to make the little decisions that define who she is, as an individual, and not part of a relationship. She decided to choose the kind of vegetables she liked rather choosing the kind that her former partner liked. This is such a simple act, yet it is where it all started.

Julia says, "Every day I ask myself honestly, "How are you doing?"

Julia recognized that she needed to take time to discover what it was she liked and disliked. She needed to learn what made her sad and what made her happy. Julia's journey was one of hope, coping, and learning to live a healthy lifestyle, which included staying focused.

Establish Boundaries

Many codependents have a very hard time saying no to anyone that asks them to do something, whether they have time or not, whether it interests them or not, whether they feel it is morally right or not… you get the picture. For you as a codependent saying 'no' is about as daunting as getting your wisdom teeth pulled. One of the best things and most important things you will do, is learn to stop being a people pleaser. You need to learn how to discover your personal boundaries and then you need to live by them.

A basic personal boundary would be that you are able to say no, when it is appropriate, and being able to draw the line. For example, you would not let your partner, convince you to do something that you did not agree with. Another example might be, you say no even though your partner is manipulating you with negative remarks.

Remember – you cannot change what other people think, nor can you change how they respond, but you can change you. Setting and enforcing boundaries is an excellent place to start.

Learn to Listen and Follow Your Intuition and Feelings

If you grew up in a dysfunctional family and you became codependent then you likely learned how to feel shame and guilt at a very young age. As a result, as an adult you need to learn how to say sorry and truthfully explain why you feel the way you, where you no longer have to do something just because it is expected of you by your partner or someone else.

Once you come out of the very restricted world you grew up in and lived in as an adult, you can start to take ownership of how you feel. It's exhilarating and freeing. No longer are you worried about what someone else thinks or feels. For the first time in your life, you come first.

Study how you feel and don't forget to remind yourself that you are free to have your own judgments, opinions, and feelings. Learn to listen to those feelings and your intuition (gut feeling) and follow it when it makes sense to do so.

Honor Your Needs

Growing up, in a dysfunctional home as a codependent you likely made your decisions based on what your parents or other family members wanted. Your decisions were never for the betterment of you. Many codependents have an impending feeling of fear before they even say a word. This behavior carried on and into your adult relationships.

Now is the time for change. For you to be aware of what you are actually feeling is healthy. To do this you need to start to question the intent behind your words and actions. By doing so you will begin to understand your motives and ideas, rather than allowing others to define them for you. It will help you to develop your self-respect and confidence and you will find it easier to communicate your needs to others.

Remember to always first honor your needs before you honor the needs of those around you.

Create a Positive Space

When you feel responsible for the thoughts and actions of those around you, along with how they react, it drains you, and often it will confuse you. It is time to learn the difference between supporting someone and owning their problems. You need to start to create a positive space around you. This has plenty to do with the boundaries you set, which we talked about earlier. You need to define where another person ends and you begin. This is also very important in your relationship with your partner.

There is no need for you to take responsibility for others. For example, if your partner hasn't called you back after three tries of calling him/her over whether or not you are meeting for dinner; it's not your fault or responsibility to make sure they act appropriately. If your friend is involved in something with his/her friends that you do not find morally acceptable, but legally, there is no need for you to step in and try to change things. You can have honest conversations, but at the end of the day, you are not responsible for your partner.

If you want to create a positive space, you need to accept the way others are, with all their flaws, and work with the pieces that are given to you, not try to make things work for them. It's not your job to take on their life. As a friend or partner, your job is to be there if they need support. Your job is also to create a positive space where you define what is acceptable and what is not acceptable in your bubble.

Commit to Lift Up Your Self Esteem and Love Yourself

A wise man once said that the more you know who you are and what it is you want; the less things will upset you. No other statement could be truer than that! What a great way to focus on what it is you need from your life.

We all make mistakes, some of us more than others. Some of us also learn faster than others from our mistakes, while others might have to repeat the lesson a few times. You need to learn first to love yourself, as you are, with the mistake you have made, and the mistakes you will make in the future.

You need to stop making negative comments about yourself, no matter how small they are. Learn to love who you are. You are a unique individual. There is not another you. Be kind to yourself. Doing all of this will help to lift up your self-esteem.

At the end of the day, you are the only one responsible for your happiness. If something makes you sad, breaks you down, harms you in any manner, attacks your self-esteem, you have the right to walk away. You might be surprised just how powerful it can be to walk away from a relationship, not knowing where you will go or how you will survive. You discover you are smart, and can take care of yourself. You discover you are stronger than you ever imagined.

Don't ever let anyone attack your self-esteem. Stand up for 'you,' because you are as valued on this planet as any other human is. Most of all, do not allow yourself to beat up your own self-esteem. Often, we are our own worst enemy.

Chapter 19: Types Of Boundaries

So we have established the foundation for creating boundaries. To take responsibility for yourself as an individual and create a self-esteem that rests on that solid foundation of self, unable to be influenced by external events.

What does this mean in practice? Several types of boundaries exist to complement each area of life. We have listed the most common sorts of boundaries below for you to consider:

Material Boundaries

As we discussed above codependents have a tendency to want to give gifts to secure approval. In their role as a care giver they may support their partner with money in times of need or indeed with any material goods they feel that person is lacking.

It is important therefore to set material boundaries. Consider carefully your motivation behind lending your possessions. Is it to gain approval of the recipient? Has that person actually asked for your support or are you giving them goods because **you** think they need them? Whilst generosity is a kind trait to have you must put boundaries in place to keep it in check and prevent abuse. For example if you are to lend money, set out clearly your expectations for repayment and enforce those terms.

Physical Boundaries

In an attempt to avoid confrontation and due to the close nature of codependent relationships you may feel you have surrendered your own personal space. For example, you might have moved in too quickly with someone or they may demand your physical presence and heap on guilt if this expectation isn't made.

Physical boundaries are an important part of independence. By having time and space to yourself it is easier to define yourself as an individual. Everyone needs some time alone to pursue things they enjoy in order to enrich their own lives.

This does not mean becoming a hermit but it is important to set aside time and space that is your own. Perhaps this might be as small as having a desk where you can work on your own artwork, or a time in the day when you can have a room to yourself. If a partner is demanding your time constantly you must be firm with them and allocate time for your own pursuits as well as spending time with them.

Mental Boundaries

Again in order to avoid disagreements or incurring the disapproval of others a codependent may abandon their own ideals to conform. It is important to form your own beliefs and ideals about the world.

Whilst you should always consider other points of views to your own if you do not find their argument persuasive you should feel free to assert your own views. This does not need to be in an aggressive fashion but it is important to stay true to yourself and not be easily persuaded. Have an open mind and consider other's opinions evenly. If you stay true to your own values you will not incur the guilt, often associated with codependents, by abandoning them.

Emotional Boundaries

As codependent's self worth is so inherently tied to the reactions and emotions of their partners, codependents can find their own mood contingent on their partner's. It is important to recognize your own emotions and not to embrace another's as your own. By taking on other worries for yourself it will not only cause you stress but will take away their own self-control, leaving them vulnerable.

Of course you should be supportive to a partner but by creating emotional boundaries you can help them through emotional times by providing support and letting them work through the problems themselves. This allows them to take control of their own lives and maintain their own autonomy.

Sexual Boundaries

At the very core of the causes of codependency is that sufferers often have no example of how to effectively pursue the affection that they desire. This often leads sufferers to mistake sexual attention as affection. Due to their low self-esteem sufferers may even accept this attention as a substitute for the love they are looking for.

Whilst physical intimacy is an important part of a relationship it should not be the fundamental component to it. You should feel free to express what you feel comfortable with and set clear boundaries of what you find acceptable and what you do not. It is important of course to take your partner's own feelings into account but equally they must understand and accept your own boundaries.

Innate Respect

These boundaries are learned from examples set early in our lives. If boundaries were violated or dismissed as a child then it is unlikely that you will maintain then as an adult. Of course any kind of abuse in childhood will leave mental and physical boundaries broken, however this doesn't necessarily mean a severe level of abuse was experience. Many children suffer bullying to lesser and greater extents during their schooling.

For example, another pupil continually throws paper at your back in class. When you express your discomfort at this, you are teased. This will teach children to shy away from expressing discomfort when their physical boundaries are tested. This may not extend to very serious breaches of physical boundaries but it will still have an effect that will pervade the adult's life.

It is important to remember that you are a dignified individual with an innate, inviolable right to respect. You have control in your life and the right to disagree with the demands set upon you. In daily activities you should be able to refuse a dinner invitation, be treated with respect at work or decline a request.

All of us are guilty of agreeing to things we'd rather not do due to social pressure. We often attend engagements where we'd rather be at home with a cup of tea and Netflix. You may find it helpful to write down some situations you've been in recently and why you accepted them instead of saying no. Write down what prevented you for asserting your rights in that situation.

Sometimes we must accept things we would rather not do, such as performing a task for your boss at work. However, is the same true of accepting the extra work of a co-worker? Could you in fact politely decline and ask your co-worker to respect the fact you also have you own work?

By respecting you own wants and needs you can consider them as more important factors in making decisions. For example, before when a co-worker asked you to perform tasks your considerations might have been fear of reprisal by the co-worker, or a need to validate yourself through their approval. Now you should feel that you can take your own feelings into account. Again ask yourself is this necessary? Will the consequences of refusal be more damaging than the actual cost to myself by doing this task? Factor your own needs as an important and weighty matter in making decisions.

Boundaries of Self

The above boundaries are tools you can use to help set out limits to your interactions with external forces. They will help you maintain respectful and fulfilling relationships at work and home.

However we must also learn to set boundaries for ourselves. This can help your self-discipline and help manage your emotions and behaviors. Neglecting internal boundaries is more difficult to detect, however it may be reflected in sufferers' inability to finish projects, procrastination or neglect of their physical needs. By taking accountability for your actions you can begin to motivate yourself better.

Instead of blaming external forces you will be able to take responsibility for your actions. For example instead of thinking 'it's too cold out to go the gym' take responsibility of the fact that you are just making excuses to yourself. Remind yourself nothing will get done if you keep making excuses. Instead of the negatives, think of all the positives you will achieve if you ignore the barriers. For example I think of the benefits of not having to take twenty minutes to fit myself into my jeans in the morning!

Conclusion

Hopefully, this book has empowered you to keep making these big, powerful strides. It's important you remember that codependent relationships are not a life sentence; relationship coaches and psychologists everywhere agree that codependencies can, indeed, be healed with time. By adhering to the helpful rules and tips in this book, you'll soon see your relationship in a whole new light. You'll be a happier, more fulfilled individual and your relationship will blossom in turn. What's important is that you continue to persist and remain self-aware.

We've covered the in-depth details of codependency, identifying what it really means and what exactly makes it different to everyday dependence on our loved ones. It's important that you recognize this distinction as there's no need to eliminate all of your dependent behavior – some of it is perfectly normal. By now, you're well aware of the difference between the two.

Codependent behavior doesn't mean never depending on our partner. It simply means having a healthy level of dependence and knowing who you are without your partner.

Before you move forward, it's essential that you figure out which codependent partner you are. Are you the enabler or the enabled? Try to approach this question without any denial. We've covered the likely backgrounds of each partner and it's possible you saw yourself in those descriptions. Perhaps you were even able to pinpoint the exact relationship in your childhood that gave you this codependent mindset. Now that you've finished this book, try and work through those memories. Which early relationship taught you to be codependent? Delve deeply into yourself and recognize that this early relationship was likely very dysfunctional. Treating your relationship the same way will only result in the same dysfunctions. You don't want that, do you? Of course not.

Once you commit to change, you'll need to start laying down some boundaries. This means saying 'no' and setting some rules where necessary. It means conveying to your partner, in some way, that you'll no longer be fixing every little thing that goes wrong. Doing this can be difficult, especially since you're not used to it. You may even have feelings of guilt or uncertainty around how to enforce them. Pay close attention to the tips we've covered and you'll soon see boundaries as completely natural. You'll suddenly find yourself with far more energy, now that you're no longer exhausted from over-exerting and doing more than your fair share.

Aside from this, it's also important that you and your partner work on building your sense of self. This may mean developing stronger self-esteem and self-awareness. Using the affirmations and exercises in this book, you can begin rewiring your psyche to produce more positive thoughts about yourself. How can you make the most of your gifts and positive qualities if you never realize they exist? Whether you realize it or not, self-esteem is a big part of healing codependency. You need to recognize that you are enough and that you are wonderful, even without a partner at your side. By creating a more positive inner dialogue, you'll help your relationship thrive.

After learning about boundaries and developing self-esteem, you were faced with some big challenges. Namely, destructive behavior. Hopefully, you were motivated and inspired to finally eliminate these harmful habits from your life. You can't evolve if you don't get rid of the obstacles. Once you've identified what these obstacles are, you can work hard on moving past them. Now that you understand the cycle of narcissistic abuse, you can hopefully recover from any abuse you've endured. If you're staying in a relationship with a narcissist, hold on tight. It may be a turbulent ride. Turn back to the section on narcissistic abuse and do your best to enact the changes that were listed – otherwise, you may find yourself stuck in a cycle that never ends. Remember this: if you don't change, nothing will!